THE WORD THAT CHANGED A NATION

FERNANDO VILLALOBOS

ASÍ LO PROMETIÓ
As He Promised

During the revival in Bolivia, God gave Julio Ruibal this promise: "Bolivia, Bolivia, small amongst nations, from you will come forth the Light of the world."

Julio came to understand that Jesus never lies, and He always fulfills His promises. He used this phrase, "Así lo prometió" often to express his trust in Jesus. His first radio and TV programs were titled *Así Lo Prometió*.

To me, this was the **word** that changed a nation. Through this phrase, we began to believe and witness the fulfillment of God's promise for Bolivia—the divine work that He would accomplish.

—Fernando Villalobos

WHAT PEOPLE ARE SAYING ABOUT THIS BOOK

I saw the evidence of the Bolivian revival during four visits I made to that country in recent years. But it wasn't until I met Fernando Villalobos in 2013 that I began to understand the incredible power that was unleashed during that move of God in the 1970s. Fernando was in the middle of a supernatural visitation, and he still carries the freshness and the humility of it. When he tells stories from those miraculous days, my heart leaps, and my eyes water. The story of how God touched Bolivia is a story that needs to be repeated today. So I pray that this book will spread that holy fire. Bolivia was changed in a matter of months when the fire swept from La Paz to Cochabamba to Santa Cruz. I pray that the same fire will spread across our nation!

J. Lee Grady
Author, Set My Heart On Fire
Director, The Mordecai Project
LaGrange, GA

Jesus Christ is the same yesterday, today, and forever. His love for people has never changed. His desire to save, heal, and transform is the same today as it was 2000 years ago. But, too often, the dearth of these things in our ministries leads us to lose hope that God is still willing to do through us the greater things of which Jesus spoke.

No matter where or when we live, revival is our desperate need. And yet, believing God and persevering in prayer until it comes is one of the most difficult callings in life. As someone who has long prayed for such things, I've often grown discouraged.

For many years, my friend Fernando has told me bits and pieces about the revival that swept through Bolivia in the early 1970s. His memories have always left me with a longing to know more. For me, this book fills in many of the gaps and gives me a much more complete account of what may be the most under-reported revival of the 20th century.

The accounts in this book are stirring. The insights are profound. Even more, what lies within these pages is an opportunity for God to renew in all of us the hope and trust that He stands ready to do it again—even through the likes of us.

Bob Beckwith
Director, University of Georgia Wesley Foundation
Athens, GA

I've known Fernando for almost ten years now. He is a dear friend and mentor to me. His humble heart and obedience to God have always inspired me and offered an example of what a life laid down for Jesus Christ looks like. I know of no one who honors, reveres, and loves Holy Spirit more than Fernando. He delights and rests in his identity as a son of God. Fernando does not seek the limelight, nor to make his name great, so I know this book is birthed from the heart of God. I thank God for Fernando's influence in my life.

Much of the content of this book has been shared with me in conversations with Fernando over the years, and I'm so excited that it is now in book form and available to a wider audience. What God did in Bolivia He wants to do again, and on an even grander scale. I wept and smiled as I read this book, weeping as I longed for God to bring revival to my nation and city, smiling as I read the testimonies of God's awe-inspiring goodness.

There is an impartation of grace, hunger and the fire of God when you read this book. 2 Corinthians 11:3 states, "But I am afraid that, as the serpent deceived Eve by his craftiness, your minds will be led astray from the simplicity and purity [of devotion] to Christ." My prayer is that God would use this book to return us to the simplicity and purity of devotion to Christ and for our hearts to be fully surrendered to Holy Spirit's leading as He brings glory to Jesus and the Father through us.

May Holy Spirit use this book to pour out fresh fire upon you. "...For the testimony of Jesus is the spirit of prophecy" (Revelation 19:10).

Travis Gay
Pastor, The Awakening
Athens, GA

I met Fernando when we were both ministering in Mexico, and we sensed an immediate bond of friendship as well as a common passion for a fresh move of the Holy Spirit. Fernando has often shared with me about some of the things that he experienced in Bolivia, so I was very excited to receive a copy of the script to read. As you read through the pages of this book, I can assure you of its authenticity because I know the integrity of the man.

The pages are filled with the amazing experiences of young people who were so inexperienced that when they read what the Bible said, they assumed that God would do what He said - and He most certainly did! It is like reading the Book of Acts, and why should it not be? Jesus Christ is the same yesterday, today, and forever. I have been inspired, in a fresh way, to trust God for miracles through my own ministry, and I trust it will do the same for you.

Fernando also reflects on the days we are living in and suggests how we can best prepare for the things that are coming as we await the imminent return of the Lord Jesus Christ. Let us take note and not be unprepared. Thank you, Fernando, my friend, for this timely and inspiring book.
Mike Knott
Former Senior Pastor, Elim International Church
Wellington, New Zealand

Copyright © 2020 Fernando Villalobos
ISBN: 9781070634913
Library of Congress Control Number: 2019909398
Published in the United States of America

All rights reserved as permitted under the U. S. Copyright Act of 1976. No part of this publication may be reproduced, distributed, or transmitted in any form or by any means, or stored in a database or retrieval system, without the expressed written permission of the author and publisher.

Unless otherwise indicated, all scripture quotations are from the ESV® Bible, *The Holy Bible, English Standard Version*®, copyright © 2001 by Crossway, a publishing ministry of Good News Publishers. Used by permission. All rights reserved.

Scripture quotations marked HCSB®, are taken from the *Holman Christian Standard Bible*®, Copyright © 1999, 2000, 2002, 2003, 2009 by Holman Bible Publishers. Used by permission. HCSB® is a federally registered trademark of Holman Bible Publishers.

Other scripture references are taken from the following sources: Holy Bible, *New International Version*®, NIV® Copyright ©1973, 1978, 1984, 2011 by Biblica, Inc.® Used by permission. All rights reserved worldwide; *New King James Version*®. Copyright © 1982 by Thomas Nelson. Used by permission. All rights reserved; *Holy Bible, New Living Translation*, copyright © 1996, 2004, 2015 by Tyndale House Foundation. Used by permission of Tyndale House Publishers, Inc., Carol Stream, Illinois 60188. All rights reserved.

Published by
Burkhart Books
Bedford, Texas
www.BurkhartBooks.com

DEDICATION

This book is dedicated to honor the name of the One who gave His life for us—the One who resurrected and lives forever, sitting at our Father's side in glory, interceding for us—our Lord Jesus Christ.

ACKNOWLEDGMENTS

First of all, I would like to recognize the patience and loving-kindness of the Holy Spirit. He is the One who inspired the writing of this book. He gave us guidance, knowledge, and boldness. The glory and the honor and the recognition are only for our Lord Jesus Christ.

I would also like to thank my wife, Laura, and the rest of my family for their support, prayers, and for the patience and advice that they have for me. To my good friend, Leopoldo Gonzalez, for his contribution of information that we used. He is a wonderful brother and always willing to help and to glorify the name of our Lord Jesus Christ.

I would also like to recognize, with much appreciation, the hard work and long hours that Lauren Steffes contributed in helping me put this story in writing and Christine Kieti for proofreading and editing the draft. They were patient, kind, and sensitive enough for the Holy Spirit to guide us through this endeavor.

CONTENTS

Así Lo Prometió - As He Promised
Dedication
Foreword   13
Prologue   15

PART I: REVIVAL IN BOLIVIA

CHAPTER 1: HUMBLE BEGINNINGS   19
CHAPTER 2: THE RIVER OF THE HOLY SPIRIT   35
CHAPTER 3: THE RIVER RISES   53
CHAPTER 4: A CHURCH IS BORN   57
CHAPTER 5: THE EXPLOSION   63
CHAPTER 6: ALL-CONSUMING FIRE   69
CHAPTER 7: A SPIRIT-BORN CHURCH   79
CHAPTER 8: THE SIMPLE GOSPEL   81
CHAPTER 9: THOUSAND-YEAR DAYS ('71-'73)   83
CHAPTER 10: WARNINGS   89
CHAPTER 11: THE DESERT: THE COST OF DISOBEDIENCE   93
CHAPTER 12: THE POISON OF LEGALISM   99
CHAPTER 13: GOD'S HOPE FOR BOLIVIA   103

Photo Gallery   113

Part II: LESSONS LEARNED

CHAPTER 14: PERSONAL LESSONS   125
CHAPTER 15: FROM UNITY TO DIVISION   137
CHAPTER 16: THE CHURCH IS ONE   141
CHAPTER 17: GRACE UPON GRACE—WALKING IN THE SPIRIT   145
CHAPTER 18: SONSHIP OVER SERVITUDE   151
CHAPTER 19: THE PRESSURE IS OFF   157
CHAPTER 20: THE REALITY OF THE CHURCH   161
CHAPTER 21: THE CHALLENGE OF GOD TO HIS CHURCH   175

Bibliography   181

About the Authior

FOREWORD

I first met Fernando decades ago, a few months after the revival had its last meeting in La Paz, Bolivia. My impression of him was that he had a deep relationship with Jesus and that he was amongst the top leadership of the movement. The next time I spoke with him was more than thirty years later after a pastor friend reconnected us.

As I got to know him, I came to the conclusion that God had preserved him as one of the few people (if not the only one) who kept himself living under the anointing and relationship with God from the revival of 1972. That is why I call him the "living relic of the revival."

Not many can write with authority regarding such a powerful event, not only as a witness but also as a protagonist. Fernando does this with a masterful description of what I call "the revival of teenagers" that God used to change a nation.

Many of the miracles and details in his book are unique, firsthand accounts, provided with deep understanding and insight into God's heart in a skillful way. Fernando shares what happened and explains why it happened.

The fact that God took Fernando away from Bolivia at the very moment at which the revival was under attack is a powerful message to the present generation, leaving a testimony of what God has done as evidence that everything we read is not only true but replicable. Reading this marvelous account of such a revival provides tremendous motivation to seek God in this generation for another visitation.

Fernando is not only writing about the history of the revival in Bolivia, he is writing about his present lifestyle and about the work of God that can change a nation, even today.

Fernando is not a pastor. He is not an evangelist. He does not travel under a title that defines him. He is a living witness of a powerful visitation that changed a nation, and, as such, he is a seed that God is willing to sow into the lives of any hungry and thirsty children seeking an awesome manifestation of God's touch to a world that desperately needs one.

The reader will be motivated, challenged, and inspired to seek God for another visitation like the one in Bolivia.

Carlos Penaloza
Senior Pastor, Ekklesia USA
Washington D.C.

PROLOGUE

The book that you have in your hands is the story of what God has done in my country, Bolivia. We are witnesses to the power, love, and mercy of God. We also got to know, in a very personal way, who the Holy Spirit is. Without Him, nothing that happened in Bolivia would have. This book would not exist. Because of His help, guidance, strength, and wisdom, this story is coming to light.

This book chronicles the work of the Holy Spirit to glorify the name of our Lord Jesus Christ in the country of Bolivia. Our prayer and hope are that it will, in some way, convey the wonderful things that He did. It is with great fear and, at the same time, excitement that we follow the Holy Spirit as He speaks through this book.

This story is intended to challenge our lives and faith, as well as to guide us in the right direction. You will see through the chapters how God's plan for Bolivia unfolded and how it affected my country that went from very few believers to hundreds of thousands of believers.

In reality, history changed for my country and the rest of Latin America. This doesn't surprise me because I know that we have a God who is powerful. We have a God who holds the universe in His hands.

For Him, nothing is impossible.

My hope and my prayer are that this book will be a blessing to your life. I know that Jesus is the same and has not changed. He continues to pour out His Holy Spirit through miracles and wonders that happen everywhere in the world.

Jesus is coming very soon, and I know that the Holy Spirit is very busy preparing the Church to be ready.

Our King is coming soon.

PART I:
REVIVAL IN BOLIVIA

CHAPTER 1

HUMBLE BEGINNINGS

But God has chosen the foolish things of the world to put to shame the wise, and God has chosen the weak things of the world to put to shame the things which are mighty. And the worst things of the world, and the things which are despised, God has chosen. And the things which are not to bring to nothing the things that are, that no flesh should glory in His presence.

1 Corinthians 1:27-29

These are verses that will never change because God does not change. He remains the same.

In the 1970s, God chose Bolivia, one of the poorest countries in the world. Bolivia is a small country in the middle of South America, a country that was not influential in the world at that time. He used a young man, Julio César Ruibal, who was just 19 years old.

Julio did not receive any formal preparation. He did not go to Bible college. He was not a pastor nor a minister. He was a young believer living in the United States who was planning and studying to be a physician. But God had other plans for him—and for Bolivia.

Julio was born in Bolivia in the city of Sucre in 1953. From a young age, Julio wanted to have a relationship with God, so he was very active in the Catholic Church. He was very impressed with a movie that he saw when he was young. This movie is called *Marcellino Pan Vino*. This movie is about an orphan who was adopted by some priests in Spain. This boy, Marcellino, used to go to the attic of a church that housed many statues of Christ. The boy loved one particular statue—Christ crucified on a cross.

One day, Marcellino went to the attic and started to talk to this man who was crucified. This man came to life. He came off from the cross and began to spend time with Marcellino, and Christ became a friend to this young boy. This movie is all about that relationship.

Julio was very impressed with the theme of the movie and began to search for spiritual truth in his life. He was longing to find that friend, to find the Jesus who was alive, but he couldn't find anything.

He went to Catholic schools. He went to mass. His search continued through his teenage years. And he became discouraged because he couldn't find what he was looking for. He resorted to yoga, the occult, and other Eastern religious practices. In his book, *Anointed for the End Times Harvest*, Julio speaks about his loss of interest in empty religious practices.

> Since my teenage years, I had been interested in the supernatural. Disenchanted with Catholic traditions, I became involved in yoga, mysticism, and the occult. Supernatural healings were often talked about in the occult, but we would seldom see any (Ruibal 18).

Julio wanted to be a doctor because he was moved by the suffering of the many sick people he encountered throughout his life. His dream was to have a boat and go through the rivers of the jungle assisting and healing people.

In *Satan on the Loose* by Nicky Cruz, Julio shares his testimony and explains how he first got involved in the occult and how those experiences affected his life before and after turning to Jesus.

> I saw no way to make my dream come true, and by the time I was eighteen years old, I had no outstanding success in anything, and everyone in my family let me know it. I tried music and sports, but I wasn't really good at either one. I felt if I couldn't change my life somehow, I would be a nothing, and I just couldn't go on living (Cruz 132).

He decided to study medicine and to investigate the occult.

> Deciding that occultism would bring me satisfaction and success, I studied it in many forms. I began with the occult religions of Tibet. These religions work basically with the control of the mind—astral projection, psychometry, telepathy, and astrology.
>
> Quickly mastering these, I went on to the religions of India, especially Hinduism and Yoga—Hatha-Yoga, Jnana-Yoga, Bhakti-Yoga, and all their variations. Then I went into the occult studies of the Western Hemisphere—palmistry, tarot

> cards, Transcendental Meditation, extrasensory perception, parapsychology. Finally, I studied what is supposed to be the highest discipline of all—the mysticism of prayer and worship.
>
> Prayer and worship sound fine, don't they? But you can pray to Satan as well as to Jesus. And you can get answers from Satan! Of course, if you pray to any spirit but the Spirit of God or Jesus, you will have to pay a price. Satan can give a person many things—money, healing, knowledge, protection, luck. Satan is a giver—but a dirty giver.
>
> What Satan gives, I have found, he always takes back with heavy interest. He is just like a drug pusher. A pusher might give you a nice free shot of dope, and for a little while you may get what you think is a wonderful high, but those few minutes or hours are followed by torment, fear, the feeling of being lost, the desperation of not knowing what is happening to you. And the pusher makes you pay a horrible price in the end—always with money—often with your life. The Bible calls Satan the Tormentor. That is the perfect description. He gives—but he takes everything back, and you have to pay a terrible interest (Cruz 133).

In 1971, with the medical dream in mind, he went to the United States, arrived in Florida, and moved all the way to California. While there, he continued with his yoga activities and began training a group of young people.

> While I was still in my teens, the doors all opened for me to come to the United States to study medicine. Very soon I was taking a premed course in Los Angeles, but at the same time, I was doing things no normal person could do. I could hypnotize people, control them with my eyes, make them do things I willed them to do. I knew things that would happen in the future. I could cause strange things to happen. I could communicate by telepathy, even if the other person were miles away. And I could learn what I needed to without studying.
>
> The work I now did was dangerous and complicated. In a few months, I had trained about fifteen students to the point where they could teach and study at the same time (Cruz 134).

By this time, he was a master in yoga.

> I advanced in the occult sphere so fast that I soon became the youngest guru in the Western Hemisphere and one of the most advanced and powerful.
>
> Twice a week, I taught yoga on television. Hatha-yoga sounds like a nice simple set of exercises; everybody thinks it is just gymnastics. I want to warn that it is just the beginning of a devilish trap. After I became an instructor in Hatha-yoga, my guru showed me that the only thing those exercises really do is open your appetite for the occult. They are like marijuana—they usually lead you onto a drug that is worse and stronger, binding you so completely that only Christ can deliver you (Cruz 134).

When you come into the land that the Lord your God is giving you, you shall not learn to follow the abominable practices of those nations. There shall not be found among you anyone who burns his son or his daughter as an offering, anyone who practices divination or tells fortunes or interprets omens, or a sorcerer or a charmer or a medium or a necromancer or one who inquires of the dead, for whoever does these things is an abomination to the Lord.
Deuteronomy 18:9-12

> Many people think that occult power is just the power of the mind. This is not true. There is a point beyond which the power of the mind ends, and demonic power takes over. For example, astrology begins with pure astronomy—with the position of the stars and planets and various dates and angles. But there is a point where this kind of information ends, and interpretation must be applied to the individual person whose horoscope you are reading. This is where the astrologer senses the need for help. This help will not come from God, for He does not want us to know the future except as He reveals it. So this is where you open yourself up to demonic influence. The demons know something about the future. Satan wants you to desire that knowledge. So here the demon steps in to provide super-human aid in interpreting the horoscope (Cruz 134).

And no wonder, for even Satan disguises himself as an angel of light.
2 Corinthians 11:14

Truly it looked as though the occult was the key to my heart's desire. Actually, I had reached the point the Tibetans call "Nirvana" and the Western Occultists call "Absolute Knowledge." It was the point where I was so in tune with the demon world that I could know things and do things without any conscious effort. I got power and information directly from supernatural sources (Cruz 134).

At the same time, he started attending college, trying to obtain a degree that would allow him to go to medical school.

While I took my premedical training, I was giving occult lectures in different schools and colleges. Everything was going my way. But you know, the devil is not like the Lord. Under the devil, you never know when the magic may backfire, and things may fall apart (Cruz 135).

Julio's spiritual battle continued as he delved deeper into the occult.

I will also turn against those who commit spiritual prostitution by putting their trust in mediums or in those who consult the spirits of the dead. I will cut them off from the community.
Leviticus 20:6 NLT

This was what happened to me next. All of a sudden things started to happen that I did not understand. There were strange problems among my students. Divisions sprang up between them. Some of my students decided to drop out of the classes in yoga. One of the students was a Jewish student named Aaron. I had such complete control over my students that when Aaron came to tell me he had decided to quit, he was crying and fearful. In fact, I was sometimes called a second Charles Manson because of my power over my students (Cruz 135).

The weirdest things happened, which I won't take time now to go into. Let me just say that my nerves were terribly disturbed, and the pains I had been getting ever since I started into the occult got worse. Within a month I had to go to the doctors. They gave me some pills but said they couldn't find anything wrong with me.

I was beginning to feel very weak and helpless. The way people sometimes know such things, I knew inside that I was dying—yes, dying. I can't tell you HOW I knew it, but I knew it. When a man is dying, you expect him to get in touch with his friends. I didn't have any friends—I had been too busy for friends. I did have my students.

I called an emergency meeting of my students, and I was so weak that they had to carry me to my bed. I was still in my teens, and I was dying. The students asked me if I wanted a priest. "No," I said. I didn't want anybody. I just wanted to die in peace. The students played a record they knew I liked, I said goodbye, wrote a farewell note and lay down to die.

I felt the shadow of death. It was not a peaceful feeling! It was a strong and ugly feeling of everlasting condemnation.

I tried to take hold of the promises of the occult world. I thought about the reincarnation I had been taught all about. I told myself that my mission in life was over, and I must get ready for the next existence. Because of my occult progress, I should have been prepared for a much better life the next time—but all of a sudden, the thought didn't make any sense.

I felt I was sliding down into a place too awful for words. I had believed I was fortified against death with my special knowledge and powers, but at that point, everything around me seemed to be breaking up, and what I thought was within my reach suddenly disappeared. I felt I was falling—then I wasn't conscious of anything more.

Next morning I opened my eyes to find my students all around me. They had stayed up all night praying for me. We had so many gods in our occult studies, I didn't know who they all had prayed to, but I am sure of one thing: someone had prayed to Jesus, and He in His amazing grace had answered that prayer.

> *I opened my eyes, and I heard a voice speaking in my heart. I didn't know what the voice was then, although I know now that it was the Lord. He was saying:*
>
> *"Julio, you have one more chance, and that is all."*
>
> *I wondered what it meant—whether it was my conscience or my subconscious trying to give me a message. But I knew I had better listen.*
>
> *I slowed down. I stopped teaching and let my students take care of the work. I slowed and slowed until the work was almost dissolved.*
>
> *As I was dismantling the work I had labored so hard to build up, I felt power working through me that was new and different. I thought this was the power of my mind, but I was wrong. I remember that when I was releasing the students, I told them, "You are free," and I felt a great relief. I, too, felt free. Something was working within me that was different from anything I had experienced before, causing me to undo all I had been doing joyfully. Naturally, the devil didn't like it!*
>
> *I felt low. The headache I had been having came back worse than ever, and everything was terrible. Things got worse and worse (Cruz 136-137).*

That was the time that God decided to intervene.

One day, Julio was with his friends outside the college, and a young lady passed by. What was unusual is that this young lady was wearing a poncho, which is a typical garment from Bolivia.

So, Julio asked her, "Is that poncho from Bolivia?"

The young lady turned around and replied, "Yes," and kept on walking.

Julio had an urge to go talk to her. He said to his friends, "I need to talk to that girl."

Obviously, his friends laughed at him and said, "You're always after girls."

Julio said, "No, there's something different about her." So he took off running to talk to her again.

Once he caught up to her, she turned to him and asked, "How did you know I am a believer?"

He said, "I didn't know. I asked you if that poncho was from Bolivia."

She responded, saying, "That's strange because I heard you ask, 'Are you a believer?'"

There you see the hand of God because normally there would not be any confusion between two questions that are totally different.

> *I was no more than three yards away from her. I know I have an accent, but not so bad an accent that what I asked could sound like, "Are you a believer?" I remember that I had pointed to Cathy's poncho as I asked my question.*
>
> *God had let her hear, not what my mouth was saying, but what my heart was asking. When I got into the occult, I was searching desperately for I didn't know what. Now I know that underneath it all, I was searching for God (Cruz 138).*

She invited him to a Christian meeting, where the healing evangelist, Kathryn Kuhlman, was going to be ministering. When Julio and his friend arrived, they could not believe their eyes. They saw a multitude of people and a choir and orchestra singing beautiful songs to God with many sick people sitting in the front row.

Kathryn Kuhlman came, and Julio described her as a "beautiful woman, wearing a beautiful dress." She appeared to be floating as she stepped on the stage. She spoke in simple terms about the love of Jesus Christ and how He died on the cross to save mankind from sin. Suddenly, the whole atmosphere changed. Miraculous power erupted, and the sick began to get healed.

> *Her voice seemed to enunciate the words carefully. Healings began to take place. A young blind boy with his head completely shaved sat in front of me. He had been operated on for a cancerous brain tumor that had caused his blindness. Right there in front of me, he received his sight. His mother cried out loud and finally fainted with shock and emotion (Ruibal 18).*

> *When we saw people being delivered from all kinds of sickness and problems, we blew our minds. All around us, people were getting visibly healed and healed and HEALED! We did not believe such a thing was possible. For the first time, the real and true power of God, the power of the Holy Spirit, got through to both of us.*

> *I had been working in healing before I came to the Lord. I searched desperately for things to help the sick—hypnotism, magnetism, all kinds of psychic therapy—but it wouldn't work. Some of us did get a few results once in a while. The devil may heal someone once in a while because what he really wants, and will do anything to get, is that person's soul, but healing is really against his nature, just as it is the essence of God's nature to heal and restore (Cruz 139).*

> *What seemed to be the most incredible thing about the service was that after so many healings had taken place, Kathryn added, "The most important thing today is yet to happen. Nobody move, nobody leave this auditorium. If you have not given your life to Jesus, you are missing the most important miracle. Our bodies, well or sick, are all going to be destroyed by death. But the soul that is saved by His power, through the new birth, is eternal" (Ruibal 18).*

Julio was in shock. He had never, ever seen anything like this in his life. Finally, he had found the thing he had been searching so much for—Jesus healing His people.

He said, "I saw the Gospel preached and demonstrated at the same time."

For the kingdom of God does not consist in talk but power.
1 Corinthians 4:20

He came to the front and opened his heart to Jesus Christ. He was also healed of a problem that he had with his back.

> *The Lord came into my life, delivering me from satanic oppression, giving me purpose, and healing all my diseases (severe migraine headaches, back problems, and deteriorating eyesight) and restoring my soul. Truly there is no other way—Jesus is the only way (Ruibal 19).*

For the second time that night, he was in shock. But he was saved.

> Although bewildered by what I had seen at that service where God's glory was manifested in such a wonderful way, I proceeded to walk in this new life. Changes came quickly in my life. Having been involved with the occult, I now became aware that I had touched the ultimate reality in Jesus, the other being false (Ruibal 19).

He said, "I went to my room. I laid on the floor. I lifted up my arms, and I said, 'Jesus, I don't need anything else because I have you.'"

After that, he received the baptism of the Holy Spirit and became involved in small meetings. His life was changing very quickly.

> The next day both of us went to a small prayer meeting. There were about fifteen people there. They all got down on their knees, and everyone prayed and prayed. I prayed, too—I believed in all kinds of spirits and powers, and I prayed to them all. Fortunately, no one there realized how far from the path I was, or if they did hear what I was saying, they didn't let on that I was making pagan prayers to false gods, and they just prayed for me anyway.
>
> After about an hour there were only about ten people still there. They were laying their hands on anyone who wanted prayer. I was still having those headaches, so I said to myself, "I might as well try it." Then I said to the Christians, "Okay, you can pray for me."
>
> I sat down in the chair where they laid their hands on whoever wanted prayer, and everyone gathered around. They were young people and older people and middle-aged people.
>
> As they stood around me and started to put their hands on my head, something started to happen. I had tremendous emotions in my soul, and there seemed to be a great commotion in the room. An explosive tension was starting to build up.
>
> I know now that the Spirit of God was beginning to expose the things so deeply embedded in my soul—yoga, clairvoyance, astrology, voodoo, belief in reincarnation, the Kabbala, levitation, metaphysical healing, automatic writing, use of the pendulum, extrasensory perception, and all the rest! The powers of darkness were coming face to face with the power of God.

God was challenging the Evil One, and I was the battlefield. I sensed that each one of those occult things was represented by a different demon that had taken hold of my soul.

My body was shaking, and the room was spinning around me. I felt what seemed like a warm electric current coursing all through me, and it made my body numb. It seemed like the Lord was giving me an anesthetic before an operation. I truly believe that He did so to prevent the demons inside me from harming me when they were expelled.

At the same time, I felt the demons leaving like an electric current shooting through my body. I felt something else. It seemed like a shock of thunder coming in and shaking my whole body. I started crying out in languages I didn't understand. I was being filled with the Holy Spirit and speaking in tongues! For nearly an hour, I was crying, shaking, lifting my hands, and feeling the tremendous power that was filling me.

Of course, at first, I did not understand what was happening. Then someone came into the room and exclaimed, "You have been delivered! You are being filled with the Spirit!" Later I wondered how this could be happening if I did not understand it was happening. But the Bible says that God knows the desires of our hearts. After all my years of fruitless searching for God, it was He who found me! (Cruz 139-41).

The Lord had come into my life at a very crucial time. He rescued me from the clutches of Satan and set me apart for His purposes when I was in terrible confusion and physically sick, unable to determine what the problem was.

I was emotionally hurt and desperately grasping for answers in my life. When He came to me, I lost nothing and gained everything (Ruibal 19).

He burned all his yoga books and told his students, "We were wrong. Jesus is the only answer."

My guru and I realized that we had to burn all our occult books, just like in Acts 19. It was not easy, believe me, after we had been studying and living by these things for so long. We

> had tapes, books, pictures - occult materials worth thousands and thousands of dollars. As we were throwing them into the fire in the middle of the night, I looked through the flames at my guru on the other side. I could see the tears shining in his eyes. I went to him and said, "I know, Nero, it hurts me too."
> We were not hurt by the price of all these things in the flames; we were hurt because we had been so terribly fooled.
> "Julio," Nero said, "I must go back to South America. My wife, my children, my relatives, and hundreds of people down there got involved in the occult through me. I've got to go back and bring them to Christ."
> When I had told my students that all the things I had been teaching them were from the devil, they had become bitter against me, and for a time, I had felt bitter against my guru. It was a heavy thing to know that we had been preaching doctrines of the devil. But as we burned the books and tapes and pictures, the peace of God came upon us, and the bitterness disappeared. After we burned the occult books, the Lord led me to help my former students one by one until most of them were delivered. One by one, they were saved and baptized until they got the blessings He had given me. It was amazing to see how He worked (Cruz 141).
>
> I have told you how I used to dream of being a doctor. When I found the Lord, I gave up everything I was doing, including my premedical studies. I gave my whole life to Him. After a while, I found myself praying for people who were sick—and they would be healed! The Lord gave me back my dream and fulfilled it in a way better than I could have ever hoped or thought (Cruz 143).

Then there was another Kathryn Kuhlman meeting at the Shrine Auditorium in California. When he got to this particular meeting, the doors were already closed. Julio found himself outside with many sick people in need of healing.

While he was there, he heard God telling him, "Stand up and preach."

He hesitated at the beginning, but finally, he relented and stood up on a chair so everyone could see him.

He said, "The same Jesus that is inside the auditorium is outside here. Who wants to be healed? I'm going to pray."

Due to his appearance, no one wanted to come to him. Perhaps they thought he was crazy because of the way he was dressed, with his long hair, blue jeans, Mexican shirt, and sandals—a typical hippy from the '70s. Finally, an old man, suffering from such severe arthritis that his form was completely twisted, said, "Pray for me, young man. I want to be healed."

So Julio said, "Come to me, and I will pray."

The man could barely walk, but he pressed on and was able to get to Julio.

Julio said, "I began to pray, and as I was about to put my hands on him, this man began to scream and said, 'I'm healed! I'm healed!' and began to run all over."

When the people saw this, many more people came to him. And God began to heal them.

Due to the miracles, a commotion quickly erupted. Some of the deacons noted what was happening outside and went to Kathryn Kuhlman and said, "There is this young man praying for people outside, and people are getting healed. Should we stop him?"

Kathryn said, "No, leave him alone. God told me that He was going to raise him up."

That was the beginning of Julio's ministry. From there, he went to Canada, then to the East Coast, close to Boston. He arrived at the Boston airport without knowing where to go. He told God, "I am not going to go anywhere until You show me Your will. I don't care how long it will take."

While he was sitting in the airport and waiting on God, another young man came and sat down near him. After a while, Julio asked, "What are you doing here?"

This man said, "I don't know. But something pressed me to come and to sit here." Then he asked Julio, "And what are you doing here?"

Julio replied, "I don't know. I am waiting for God to tell me what to do."

So they laughed, and Julio said, "Well, I think we have to go together."

This man said, "Yes, I am going to take you to the Catholic Church."

When they arrived, the priest was going out of town, and they met him at the door.

The priest said, "God told me that He was going to send this young man, so we already have a room prepared for him and everything he will need. Take good care of him until I come back."

Julio was raised as a Catholic in Bolivia and had been seeking a true relationship with God since he was a little boy. He was also educated in a Catholic high school, but since he could not find what he was looking for, a sense of resentment began to grow in his heart.

Many Catholics in Boston knew about the baptism of the Holy Spirit through the revival that took place through David du Plessis in the 1960s and 1970s. In 1936, Smith Wigglesworth, a British evangelist and a patriarch of the Pentecostal movement, prophesied to David du Plessis, General Secretary of the Apostolic Faith Mission (AFM) in Johannesburg, that he would see the outpouring of the Holy Spirit across mainline denominations.

As David du Plessis began to see the fulfillment of Smith Wigglesworth's prophecy, he became known as "Mr. Pentecost." Eventually, God opened the doors to the Catholic Church, even the door for David to minister in Rome and the Vatican, which exposed Catholics around the world to the baptism of the Holy Spirit.

> In the September 9, 1974 issue of Time magazine, David was mentioned alongside such people as Billy Graham; he was one of the eleven greatest "shapers and shakers" of Christianity in the twentieth century.
> Then on November 9, 1983, David was honored with the Benemerenti Medal by Pope John Paul II, an award for outstanding service to all of Christianity. It was the first time this award had been given by the Roman Catholic Church to someone who was not a Catholic (Liardon 2018).

When God sent Julio to Boston, He had prepared a place where the priest already knew and followed the Holy Spirit.

> *And it shall come to pass afterward, that I will pour out my Spirit on all flesh; your sons and your daughters shall prophesy, your old men shall dream dreams, and your young men shall see visions.*
> Joel 2:28

In hindsight, we can see what God was doing in Julio's life through this time in Boston.

I believe God wanted to heal his heart and remove any resentment towards the Catholic church. This needed to be done because God would open the first doors to the revival and Julio's ministry through the Catholic church in Bolivia. God was restoring Julio's heart because he was going to preach in a Catholic country. The Holy Spirit was going to be poured out onto Catholics in Bolivia.

When Julio spoke, he spoke only about Jesus, the Father, and the Holy Spirit. He never mentioned denominations or religions. Catholic listeners were able to relate to that message because they knew who Jesus was, who God was, and they were about to know who the Holy Spirit was in a very personal way. At the beginning of the revival, many Catholic priests were filled with the Holy Spirit and began to understand what God was about to do in Bolivia.

La Mansión Catholic Charismatic Center in Santa Cruz was one of the places born due to the outpouring of the Holy Spirit. The church still meets 40 or more years later and is a door for the Holy Spirit to touch Catholics even now.

Julio ended up in a nice room at a Catholic church in Boston with an office and a private secretary. He was going through the school of the Holy Spirit and learning how to hear His pure and lovely voice, how to depend on Him, how to recognize His guidance and His presence. He didn't have a clue what God had in store for him. His training was intense, and his growth was supernatural. They began to have meetings. Daily, God would bring people to be healed. A revival began to take place.

After that, God told Julio that He wanted him to return to Bolivia to preach the Gospel.

CHAPTER 2

THE RIVER OF THE HOLY SPIRIT

I am always amazed how the river of the Holy Spirit begins. I am from Bolivia, and I lived most of my life in La Paz, where the really big mountains, the Andes, are.

One of my favorite things to do when I was young was to go to the jungle. In order to go to the jungle, you must first climb up to the mountains. Up in the mountains is where the rivers are born. At the beginning, a river starts with just a few drops and forms a very small stream of water. And that stream keeps growing, little by little. As the water runs down the mountain and gets close to the jungle, it becomes a river, and that river joins with other rivers that are coming down also.

At the end, the rivers form the Amazon River, the biggest river in the world—so strong that nothing can contain it. Nothing can control it. Through the years, I began to understand that the move of the Holy Spirit is like a river. It starts in very small places and gets stronger and stronger until it is such an explosion that nobody can control it.

That's exactly what happened in Bolivia.

Julio arrived in La Paz in August 1972, and he first went to his father's house.

His father was shocked to see him and said to Julio, "What are you doing here? You're supposed to be in college."

He said, "No, Dad. I am going to preach the Gospel."

Julio's father was very angry with him. He called Julio's mother and said, "We are going to put Julio in the army because that's the only thing that can teach him and change his mind."

Julio's parents were divorced and, according to Julio, could never agree on anything. But this was the first time they were in accord. When Julio found out about his parents' plan, he ran away. He had no choice. He began to look for his friends so he could live with them. His parents didn't have a clue what God was about to do with his life, and at the beginning, they did not believe in anything that Julio said. But God had a plan to change their minds.

Meanwhile, Julio was searching to figure out where he should go or who he should talk to. He thought that the best thing to do would be to go to talk to pastors. He went to talk to an association of pastors in La Paz. He began to tell them that Jesus was going to touch Bolivia, that healings were going to take place and that stadiums were going to be full of people.

To Julio's dismay, they rejected him. They told him, "You are a false prophet, and we don't believe the things that you are talking about. So get out."

They kicked him out. So he asked the Holy Spirit what to do. The Holy Spirit told him, "Go to your friends."

So he began to look again for his friends to share his experiences with them. And his friends began to open their hearts to Jesus and to receive the baptism of the Holy Spirit.

Julio said to his friends, "You tell your friends to come together so that I can share with them, and I'll tell my friends to come."

The meetings began by word of mouth, and the friends began to gather in houses. The power of God was evident because everybody was beginning to give their lives to Christ and get touched by the Holy Spirit.

Julio's message was very simple: "Jesus is alive. Jesus loves you. Jesus is coming very, very soon."

With that, the Holy Spirit did the rest. The number of believers began to grow because God began to heal people, God began to change people, and God began to do miracles amongst them.

> My ministry began with family and friends. They knew me well enough to know that something radical had happened in my life. Many were saved and formed a small nucleus of believers. As I preached to friends and relatives, God began to move with signs. People were miraculously touched by the Lord and healed. That small nucleus soon grew to 20, 50, and 100 people (Ruibal 23).

When the size of the meetings grew too large for houses, Julio had to search for larger locations. While the Evangelicals had closed the door on Julio, the Catholic church opened its doors. The first public meetings were held in a Catholic building, the Church of San Miguel in La Paz. At one of the meetings there, Julio saw his father listening and watching as he preached the Gospel.

When Julio began to pray for the sick people, there was a young boy that came for prayer. Julio saw this little boy and said, "I need a witness for what God's about to do."

So he pointed at his father and said, "You, sir, come over here and be a witness."

He didn't say or mention anything about this man being his father. So Julio said to him, "Do you see this little boy? He doesn't have ears, and he doesn't have ear canals." Everything was sealed off.

Then he said, "Now watch what God is going to do."

So he prayed, and suddenly the ears began to grow. The ear canals began to form in both ears.

Julio's father was in shock at the things he was hearing and seeing. He fell on his knees and received Jesus Christ as his savior. That, to my knowledge, was the first creative miracle that happened in Bolivia. With that, God changed Julio's father's heart.

Bolivia is a small, landlocked nation that is located in the middle of South America. Sometimes it is called the "heart" of South America and borders Peru, Chile, Argentina, Paraguay, and Brazil.

In the 18th century, Bolivia was the first colony that rebelled against Spain, the country that colonized most of Latin America. Ironically, it was the last country to declare its independence from Spain in August 1825. The history of Bolivia has been very chaotic because of political instability, social segregation, and economic poverty. Politically, during the 1940s and '50s, most of the parties ruling Bolivia had socialist and communist tendencies. At that particular time, they took over the oil and mining companies and the majority of other natural resources that controlled the economy.

As these populist parties began to evolve into dictatorships, presidents wouldn't last for more than a few months. In fact, Bolivia was famous for having the most number of presidents per year. During the '60s and '70s, Cuba's Fidel Castro and Che Guevara wanted to extend their revolution into Latin America. During this time, the Bolivian government was immersed in the fight against Che Guevara's guerrillas. The students and the people wanted to have a Communist government.

In the midst of this turmoil, Hugo Banzer Suarez came to power in 1971 as a military dictator. Economically, Bolivia was one of the poorest countries in Latin America. In his 1964 speech, General René Barrientos Ortuño, President of Bolivia at that time, said poverty levels reached close to 60 percent. Due to the socio-economic gaps, social injustice was extreme. The majority of the population was indigenous, but they were treated like slaves.

The Catholic Church had such tremendous power and influence with the government that it was recognized and sustained as the official religion of Bolivia. Other religions were able to share their beliefs, but great persecution came in the midst of this atmosphere. The Evangelical Church was almost nonexistent. From what I could see, everybody was proud to be a Catholic. Being a Protestant or an Evangelical Christian had a negative connotation, with only the poor and the uneducated identifying as such.

Without statistical data, it is hard to fathom the size of the revival in Bolivia: the numbers of people healed and saved, the ways in which my nation changed and how the church was impacted, not only in Bolivia but throughout South America. With regret, I have to understand and admit that statistics from a third-world country at that particular time are unavailable. What I can share with you are pictures from newspapers from the time of the revival.

So, I will leave it to your imagination. You be the judge.

I only know that when the Holy Spirit moves, there is nothing impossible. There is not a heart of stone that He cannot touch and break.

He is the author of Pentecost, and we were able to witness another wave of Pentecost in Bolivia. I believe that we are again about to experience the fulfillment of the prophecy found in the book of Joel, "'I will pour out my Spirit upon all flesh,' says the Lord" (Joel 2:28).

I think the next revival is going to be worldwide, and with modern technology, we are going to have all the statistics we need. We need to recognize and be grateful for all the people that prayed for the revival to come to Bolivia.

Actually, the ground was prepared with tears, sorrows, and even bloodshed by many brothers and sisters. We need to acknowledge that and give thanks to God for their lives because, without them, I don't think the revival would have come to Bolivia. There were many Evangelicals that paid the price with their lives.

In the Melcamaya massacre of 1949, in the city of Oruro, several Baptist believers were killed with stones and knives. They included two Bolivian pastors, a Canadian missionary and five Quechua brothers, two of whom were teenagers. Living as an Evangelical Christian was very difficult during the '40s, '50s, and '60s. In the midst of this background, God, in His sovereignty, decided to change this country with the Gospel.

Julio Cesar Ruibal received a prophecy shortly before leaving the US:

Bolivia, Bolivia, small amongst nations, from you will come forth the Light of the World.

I think in this book, you are going to be able to understand the magnitude of this prophecy and how it was fulfilled. Julio was just obedient to God. He did not have a plan. He did not have resources. And he did not have any preparation as to how to bring revival to a country. He knew that he had to totally depend upon the Holy Spirit and surrender everything to Him. Julio had many positive attributes, but the ones that touched my life, more than any other, were his obedience to God and how he totally surrendered to the Holy Spirit.

What began as a trickle of water began to form a small river.

Houses began to open, and friends of friends of his friends began to become believers. Suddenly, everybody was curious about Jesus. Students in high schools and universities were curious. Everybody began to talk about Jesus as if He was alive and walking through the streets of La Paz.

Healings began to take place. Miracles began to take place—not only through Julio but also through the young people that gave their lives to Jesus. Julio was the leader, and he began to teach them what the Holy Spirit was teaching him. Like in the Bible, believers were sent out two by two to different parts of La Paz: houses, squares, plazas—wherever the Holy Spirit led them.

We began meeting in homes and auditoriums. We marched in the streets, preached in the plazas, and the group grew even larger. The most dangerous gang in the nation was saved and joined us. The houses and auditoriums could no longer hold us so we would meet in parks (Ruibal 23).

The people in La Paz began to hear about Jesus through friends, families, acquaintances—even strangers. It was common-place to take a taxi and hear the taxi driver ask, "Did you hear that healings are taking place? People are talking and saying that Jesus is alive."

The same thing would happen if you went to the market. People would tell you that Jesus was alive. You could go to the bank, the pharmacy—anywhere. The atmosphere in La Paz began to change radically. Everybody was talking about Jesus, and everybody began to become very curious about who Jesus was.

I remember my own encounter with Jesus.

Like Julio, I was involved with the Catholic Church. I used to help the priest with communion. I used to go with my friends to ring the bells and call people to come to mass. I really wanted to find Jesus and was impressed by the same movie that moved Julio, *Marcellino Pan y Vino*. I wanted to have a Friend like Marcellino did. But because I couldn't find anything, I was very discouraged. In the Catholic Church, I only found religion by works, and that was it.

At the time, there was this philosophy that came from Russia, China, and other nations that were supporting a godless political agenda. The Russians believed that God was a creation of the human mind. Karl Marx, the German philosopher and economist, had said, "Religion is the opium of the masses."

Since I couldn't find any truth, I agreed with these philosophies. So I said to myself, "God doesn't exist. Everything is a farce."

At the same time, there was a lot of struggle between communism and capitalism.

The Communists used to say, "Jesus is the creation of the Americans. With that, they want to control countries."

To me, that made sense because most of the missionaries were Americans. I guess I became an atheist, and I forgot about God. What I remember is that I used to get together with my friends to play soccer, have fun, and hang out together. That was our life—just to have fun.

Suddenly, it seemed, with the atmosphere changing so much in La Paz, people wanted to do good things. So my friends got together and said, "We just get together and play soccer. Why don't we help people?"

To me, that was the strangest thing I had ever heard. Suddenly my friends wanted to help people—poor people. I looked at them like they were crazy, but I went along with them. We had a meeting at a friend's house and talked about helping people.

A few days later, I was hanging around with my friends in my neighborhood. I saw a neighbor, a girl that I wanted to take out to a movie, walking to her house.

I told my friends, "I am going to ask her to go to the movies with me."

I approached her and saw she was crying. I asked, "Why are you crying? Do you have a problem? Why are you so sad?"

She said, "No, I don't have a problem, and I'm not sad. Today is the most beautiful day of my life."

I thought to myself, "Well, perhaps she got a scholarship to go study in the United States," because that was everyone's dream at the time.

She looked at me and said, "Fernando, today is the most beautiful day of my life because I found out that Jesus loves me, and Jesus loves you. He is alive, and He is coming back very soon."

I looked at her, and I couldn't believe it. It was like someone was slapping me in the face.

I didn't say anything, but I turned back and went to my friends.

"Did you ask her out?" they asked.

"She is crazy," I told them. "She told me that Jesus is alive and that Jesus loves me." We all laughed and started making fun of her.

The next day, again in my neighborhood, I talked to a younger girl that was like a sister to me. I knew that this girl had been using drugs. At that time, LSD and marijuana use was very prevalent in Bolivia. I approached her and wanted to talk to her.

She said, "Fernando, this is the most beautiful day of my life." She was smiling and looked very happy. She was radiating happiness.

I said, "Why?"

"Because Jesus loves me, and He loves you. He is alive," she said, in practically the same words as the other girl.

I looked at her and said, "Look, I do not know what you took today, but I think you are hallucinating. You should go home and get some rest."

God began to bother me. I began to think, "Why is everyone talking about Jesus? He is not real." I began to get angry.

When I got home, my youngest brother came to me, and he said, "Fernando, do you know that Jesus is alive?"

That I couldn't take. I became so angry that I threw my shoe at him, and I said, "If I catch you, I am going to beat you up." He took off running.

Later on, he came back and said to me, "Why are you angry with me? I'm just telling you what everybody's talking about. As a matter of fact, why don't you go to one of the meetings and just see for yourself what they are talking about? Today there is a meeting close to home."

I was thinking to myself, "How is it that this kid knows so much about these things?"

It was a Wednesday in December of 1972. I was 20 years old and enrolled in university to study medicine.

When I got close to the house, I noticed many people sitting on the sidewalk about two or three blocks before the house. They were of all ages, classes, and they were so peaceful, talking amongst themselves and laughing. I passed by thinking, "Why are all these people here?"

I couldn't understand what was going on. Why were they sitting on the sidewalk, so peaceful? When I arrived at the house, the door was locked. There were so many people inside that there was no space. I asked someone how to get in, and they told me to come back Friday for another meeting. I just stood there in shock. I couldn't understand why there were so many people inside and what they were doing there.

Suddenly, they opened the door and said, "We are going to a bigger house."

I was very curious by that point, so I was determined not to miss this meeting. Once I made it inside of the house, we were packed in like sardines, shoulder-to-shoulder. Nobody was talking or speaking a single word. I kept on thinking, "What is everyone doing here?" There was no music. There was no food. There was nothing.

I asked someone, "What now?"

The person replied, "Just wait. Do you see that young man with the book tucked under his arm? He is going to speak."

I saw the speaker from the back and realized that he looked familiar to me. I actually recognized him since he was a friend of mine. He was dealing drugs and was the supplier of my neighborhood. When I saw him, I thought, "Everything makes sense. They are all happy because they are on drugs and hallucinating about Jesus."

Finally, this young man spoke. Literally, his sermon consisted of, "Who wants to know Jesus? Lift up your hands."

That was all he said.

I lifted up my hand and said, "I really want to know Jesus."

He didn't say anything to me. He recognized me. He just said, "Jesus, touch him."

The next thing I remember, I was on my knees, and I saw Jesus dying on the cross.

I could see the blood. I could see His face. I could see the pain in His eyes—so many expressions, so many details.

Suddenly, I realized that He was suffering and dying for me.

I began to tell Him, "I'm sorry, Jesus. I'm sorry. I really didn't know that You died for me." And I began to ask for forgiveness. I was crying. I didn't understand what was happening to me.

When I finally stood up, my life changed forever. Finally, I found my Friend, Someone who was alive. Someone that I could talk to and be with. That was my experience, and I think my experience was not unique to me, but the experience that hundreds of thousands of people had in my country during the revival.

Conviction of Sin

And when He comes, He will convict the world concerning sin and righteousness and judgment.

John 16:8

When my friend touched me, I was not expecting anything to happen.

At first, I felt conviction for my sin. I began to ask for forgiveness because the Holy Spirit was showing me my sins. I felt guilt and sorrow because my eyes were opened, and I saw Jesus dying for me on the cross. That blew my mind. The image was so vivid and so real that the only thing I could say was "Jesus forgive me, forgive me. I didn't know that You died for me."

I was in shock. I was awakened to good and evil. Before, I had no real conscience. Before I knew Jesus, I did not care for people. I was just living in my own world to have fun and live for myself. After I knew Jesus,

He gave me His compassion and His heart for sick people. I began to understand that Jesus died for every person, and that awakened my senses.

For the religious Catholics who had no real relationship with God, Christianity was like a mythical story. They told me that Jesus died on the cross, but the Catholics were always focused on the past. The gospels were just stories that were disconnected. Before my encounter with Christ, I would hear the Catholics talk about heaven and hell, but I had no sense of God's mercy, love, or tangible presence. At that moment, Jesus became real to me. I was finally discovering that what happened 2,000 years ago was present today because I saw Jesus dying for me, for my personal sins.

When I stood up after that experience, the thing that I noticed was that I knew that I knew that I knew that Jesus was alive. I knew that heaven was real. I knew that hell was real, and I had the sense that Jesus was coming soon—very soon. I became obsessed with Jesus. I only thought about Him, wanted to talk about Him, read about Him, and know about Him.

From that moment, hope, joy, and peace entered into my life. I was totally different to the point that when I arrived home that night, my mother got scared and asked, "What happened to you?"

As soon as I arrived back at my house, I was searching for a Bible. My mom showed me a Catholic Bible, and I began to read it, far into the night. The next morning I began to share my experiences with my friends.

I began to pray all day. I didn't play soccer or watch movies anymore. I forgot about everything. I didn't hang out with my old friends, and if I did, I just shared the Gospel. I even ended up leaving my friends because my life had changed so much, I had nothing in common with them and began to seek relationships with other new believers.

God's kindness is what led me to repentance (Romans 2:4). And that is how He worked in every heart during the revival. He revealed His love for us then showed us the sin He wished to remove from our life. We need to remember that there is no condemnation for those who are in Christ Jesus (Romans 8:1). While the Holy Spirit always convicts us, He will never condemn us. That's Satan's job as the Accuser of the Brethren (Revelation 12:10).

My life changed radically, and I began to have a relationship with the Holy Spirit.

Relationship With Julio

The day God touched me, I didn't know that my friend who prayed for me was almost at the top of the leadership God was building in Bolivia. My former drug dealer friend walked with me back to my house that day because we were friends.

I had so many questions for him. "What happened to me?"

He said, "God touched you. You know, Jesus is coming back very soon."

I said, "Really?"

He said, "Yes, it's in the Bible. You should read it."

He began to describe how Jesus would come back and what the Bible said. It was surreal. I was so impressed. He told me that we were going to have a meeting in Baden-Powell Square, which is a small plaza in the Miraflores zone of La Paz. I went to that meeting, and that was where I met some of the leadership. They were singing and speaking in an unfamiliar language.

I asked, "Can you write down whatever you are saying, so I can pray like you do?"

They said, "Those are tongues."

I said, "What are tongues?"

"Well, when the Holy Spirit touches you, He gives you a new language" (Acts 2:3).

I really wanted it.

It was in that place that they invited me to meet at Chicho's house. Chicho was at the top of the leadership.

Then they said, "Julio is going to be there."

"Where does he live?"

By then, everyone wanted to be with Julio, so they were very secretive about where to meet and what time. They gave me the address, and when I arrived and knocked, I got in, and Julio was there.

I thought, "So, this is Julio."

He was only 19 years old.

I was thinking, "Wow. So skinny. Like us. Just a hippy with long hair."

This time, however, he was wearing a suit. The Holy Spirit would always tell him what to wear.

He said, "There are a lot of needs here, but before you do anything, ask the Holy Spirit who you should pray for. He is the only One who knows the hearts of the believers."

So I began to pray and ask the Holy Spirit for whom I should pray.

The Holy Spirit told me to pray for Julio, and I said, "I don't think so. I think Julio needs to pray for me."

I had a weird conversation where I argued with the Holy Spirit. He is so persistent. Finally, I surrendered and agreed to pray for Julio.

Julio was seated in the center of the room, praying. I approached him and placed my hands over his head. I think he was surprised to see me because he grabbed me, and he started praying for me.

It was a wonderful time.

That day something came to me like a transfer. I didn't know it then, but I know now that it was an impartation of the anointing Julio had received from the Holy Spirit. After that, I didn't see him much, but a deep connection was established between Julio and I. The strange thing is that I felt as though I knew him—what his heart was like and what his needs were. I would know how Julio was feeling and what was happening to him. I had a burden to pray every day for him. And so I did. I took it as my job, my privilege to pray for him. I was very disciplined and faithful to do this.

To me, meeting Julio and becoming his friend was a miracle. So many people were talking about him and wanting to meet him. Julio began to understand the magnitude of the move of the Holy Spirit from the comments that he was making to his friends.

One day, as they were walking through the streets of La Paz, he told his friend, "In a few months, I'm not going to have this luxury of just walking through the streets of La Paz. Very soon, I will not have the privacy to do anything. I am even going to require bodyguards."

And that's exactly what happened.

Julio couldn't walk through the streets of La Paz anymore because, like Jesus, everyone wanted to talk to him, to be touched by him.

I saw Julio again before he left for Peru, and then after that, I didn't see him for the rest of the year.

Sanctification of a Nation

To me, the Christian life is not about theory but experience. You establish a relationship with the Holy Spirit. He is the One that changes your life totally. For instance, I didn't know that smoking was bad because everybody smoked cigarettes or marijuana. Nobody was telling us not to smoke. Julio was busy, the revival was already on, and there were so many young people coming to Christ. Our leaders couldn't handle every person.

We had very little human guidance, but we had a lot of spiritual guidance because the Holy Spirit began to take over our lives and teach us. In some of the meetings, because we began to love each other deeply as brothers and sisters, we began to share everything, just like the early church in the Book of Acts. We didn't have much, but what little we had, we began to share. One thing that we shared were cigarettes. In some meetings, we used to pray and then read the Bible. While we were reading the Bible, we would light up cigarettes and smoke and share them. Our meetings were full of smoke. We didn't know any better. Yet, the Holy Spirit still moved.

> *Or do you not know that your body is a temple of the Holy Spirit within you, whom you have from God? You are not your own; you were bought with a price.*
>
> 1 Corinthians 6:19-20

I knew that cigarettes were bad when the Holy Spirit told me He didn't want me smoking. One day I was reading the Bible and smoking a cigarette when the Holy Spirit told me, "I don't like that."

I said, "Well, we have a problem because I tried to quit smoking before."

My dad had scared me because, while he seldom smoked, I was smoking four packs of cigarettes a day by that time. He told me I would die of cancer if I didn't stop smoking. I had started smoking around the age of 12 and tried to quit around the age of 17, but I couldn't.

After that, I thought, "Perhaps I'm going to die of cancer." So that was my consolation.

I remember talking to Jesus and telling Him that I had tried to quit but couldn't.

"Please help me out." I broke my cigarette and threw it away.

The shocker came the next morning because I forgot about my prayer. I tried to smoke, and I couldn't. The cigarette tasted terrible. I tried three cigarettes, so I thought I had bought a bad pack. I kept grabbing new packs, and the same thing happened. I suddenly remembered my prayer—God took away my cigarettes by His grace.

Then I began to learn and understand that He is the One who changes our lives. He is the only One who can change our nature. It's not that I don't want to smoke—I can't! Once, later, I tried to smoke when I was mad at God. I knew how much He hated cigarettes. I went and bought cigarettes and tried and failed. God completely changed my nature.

That's the way I am now. I am not a perfect person, but I'm not going to fake anything. I don't try to be a holy person. Before the revival, I loved to curse, but now I can't curse anymore. I cursed so much that more than 80 percent of my vocabulary were curse words. The Holy Spirit told me that both cursing and blessing cannot come out of my mouth (James 3:10). I didn't know what to do. So I decided not to curse anymore.

That decision didn't work out well because I realized that cursing was not only in my mouth, but it was in my brain, it was in my heart. It had become part of my nature. Although I wasn't saying anything, I was thinking about it. I was still cursing but in silence. I became very frustrated, trying to correct this problem. I asked for the Holy Spirit's help.

He told me, "The name of Jesus is powerful and sufficient" (Matthew 28:18, John 14:14).

When I heard that, I thought to myself, "Every time that I think about or feel like cursing, I'm going to say, 'Jesus.'" So here I was, saying, "Jesus" all the time. My friends thought I was going crazy because, truly, I have no clue how many times a day I was repeating "Jesus, Jesus."

It became a battle. Because of how ingrained cursing was in my nature, this process took several months, perhaps more than three. To me, it felt like a long, long time, until one day, something broke inside me. It was not only a feeling, but I actually heard the sound of something being broken inside of me. It sounded and felt like when you snap a pencil in half.

That day, I was totally delivered from cursing. Cursing was no longer part of my nature. To this day, over 40 years later, I have never, ever cursed again. It is not part of me anymore. I think we are not aware of how sinful and ingrained cursing is in our nature. The only One who can deliver us from that sin is the Holy Spirit.

Now, if I hit my finger with a hammer, the only thing that comes out of my mouth is "Jesus."

He still has a lot to change in me. When He does makes a change in me, I know it, and I can give Him the glory. Nobody else can change a human (John 15:5). The problem is that as Christians, we try to help Him out. We are always trying to take the bad out of ourselves, but we can't do it. Only the grace and power of God can change our lives and bring the perfection that we will someday attain (1 Thessalonians 5:23).

Everyone began to understand the grace of God in this way. So many people were beginning to turn from various sins and problems by the grace and love of God. He truly was cleaning us, changing our nature. One day I was with a believer, a girl who was also having problems with cigarettes. She very much wanted to smoke a cigarette, so I said, "Okay, I'm going to buy you a cigarette because that's what's in your heart. The only one who can change you is Jesus."

She wanted a cigarette, so I bought her a cigarette. She started smoking and asked, "Aren't you mad?"

I said, "No. God is the only one who can take that away." I shared with her my testimony about quitting smoking.

She went home, and the next day, she came back. She said, "Fernando, it happened to me also. I can't smoke anymore."

I said, "Welcome to the club."

Suddenly, many more started to quit. There were no rules; the Holy Spirit convicted us and changed us. He simply transformed our nature.

At that time, I didn't know what grace was. All I knew was that the Holy Spirit was the only one who could change us. We didn't know the theological basis for sanctification. We were not mystics. We loved playing and had fun and laughter and joy. We could never be serious. Either we were playing or praying.

We had such a childlike faith with no condemnation.

Since we were living in the '70s, we were like all the other hippies of our day—all about maintaining "good vibes," sleeping around, smoking marijuana. But as thousands of young people came to Christ every day, He began to set apart and make us holy—even while we didn't yet know what that meant or what it looked like!

God made such radical changes in all of us. We didn't try to change or even know we needed to. Nobody can be perfect out of their own strength. The enemy will condemn you and pressure you to follow the law, but Jesus tells us to become like children (Matthew 18:3) and simply abide in His love because apart from Him, we can't do anything (John 15:5).

Just imagine—one day you don't believe in anything, and the next day you are so sure of who Jesus is, not only in words but in power! It just blows your mind! It was not about religion; it was about meeting a person and having a relationship with Him. Either you did, or you did not. You couldn't be in the middle.

Yet although God began to change our nature, we continued to dress exactly like the other hippies our age. Girls still wore their skirts short, and guys wore their bell-bottoms. Remember, the Lord does not judge by outward appearances but by the heart. He was more committed to changing our character than our clothes (1 Samuel 16:7).

Another change the Lord accomplished within the groups of young people was ridding us of sexual sin and promiscuity. Yet, instead of commanding us to follow the rules, He did so in His own way of gentleness and love by showing us how His ways are so much better than ours. My wife Laura will explain how the Holy Spirit taught us about sex, marriage, and how to regard one another as brothers and sisters in Christ.

> There were thousands and thousands of young people who had been living worldly lives. So previously promiscuous men and women were just having fun and sleeping around with one another. Since we were in the '70s, people practiced "free love."
>
> Without anyone telling us that we should not have sex with one another, the Holy Spirit took us to the Word and showed us that we were now holy. He convicted us about dating or embracing someone whom we would not eventually marry.

Drink water from your own cistern,
running water from your own wells.
Let them be only your own and not strangers with you.
Rejoice with the woman of your youth.
Proverbs 5:15-17

THE WORD THAT CHANGED A NATION

I did not want to scatter my source of life outside of marriage to any man. I was convicted to keep myself pure and holy for one man, in marriage. This happened to many young men and women.

—Laura Villalobos

Another thing that the Holy Spirit brought to us was a sense of family that many of us did not have before. Now it is very strange when I hear, "I have a Christian friend" instead of "brother" or "sister." To me, it's like family and friends are two different concepts. We saw ourselves as a family. So any Christian girl was my sister. In my mind, you don't date your sister, so I would not cross that boundary. God changed our minds very quickly, so we were protected. With that understanding, we didn't have much time to be thinking about girls and boys because we were so occupied with the things of God. All of our attention was on Jesus. We actually even forgot about our own selves. When your heart is set on God, you don't even have a sense of awareness about who you are anymore. The older Christian women were our mothers. The few older men were father figures.

In the early days of the revival, life in the Spirit was so sweet, so easy. The bondage of religion and legalism had not yet entered our lives, but it would one day soon. We would eventually see how man's attempt to attain holiness and personal perfection can lead to division, destruction, and even death.

CHAPTER 3

THE RIVER RISES

The river of the Spirit was rising, and the valley couldn't contain it anymore. Young people, old people—all types of people were giving their lives to Christ. To truly talk about the revival, we would need to write many books to describe all God did in Bolivia accurately. People were having real encounters with the Living God.

Julio's message was, "Jesus is the same. He has not changed. He is alive, so we should expect Him to do the same things He did 2,000 years ago."

That is exactly what began to happen.

Healings and miracles began to take place. We were witnesses to everything that is described in the Acts of the Apostles in the New Testament. I truly believe that the book of Acts continues to be written, because those are acts, not of the apostles, but of the Holy Spirit, using men.

When Jesus walked the earth, He had compassion on the crowds that came to hear Him speak, and that compassion has not changed. When they grew hungry, He multiplied fish and bread to feed them.

Well, in Bolivia, that began to happen. In the beginning, hundreds would attend the meetings. Since we were young, most of the people in high school or college did not have much money. We were always hungry. One day, close to 200 people came to a house, and the meetings usually lasted four to seven hours or longer. After the meeting, the owners of the house noticed that the people were hungry.

They said, "We need to feed the people. What do we have?"

They had two cans of sardines and five loaves of bread.

They said, "That's all we have, so God will have to multiply it." So they prayed to Jesus and asked Him to multiply it.

With two cans of sardines and five loaves of bread, 200 people began to eat.

During the revival, I remember how my Christian friends used to come to my house for lunch uninvited. The first time, my mother was so upset she said, "Fernando, I can't feed your friends. We just have enough food for our family."

I said, "Mom, Jesus will provide. He always multiplies food."

She looked at me like, "Have you lost your mind?"

But she began to serve the food. And she began to cry because the food just began to come out from the pan, and people simply continued eating and eating. We had half of a pan of food left over for the next day. That happened to so many people and so many families in so many places and so many cities. Witnessing the miracle of food multiplication became normal to us. It was not something so extraordinary. God truly was moving in a powerful way.

Since we were young, we would often gather at the home of a Christian woman. She was much older than us, perhaps around 40 years old, while we were in our early 20s. Berta became our spiritual mother, so she would often feed us. One day, in particular, we witnessed one of the most miraculous moves of the Holy Spirit I have experienced to this date.

It was New Year's Day, and Berta wanted to have Julio over for dinner, so she invited him. He asked, "Can I bring some people?" because Julio was always with people.

"Sure," she said, "How many?"

There were close to 20 people that he invited. Berta wanted to serve chicken. At that time, chicken was Bolivia's most expensive meat and reserved only for holidays.

When Julio made it to Berta's house, he came with more than 200 people.

Berta became very upset with him.

"Julio, how could you do this to me? I don't have enough food for everybody, and I cannot go to the market. Everything is closed. I cannot cook. I cannot do anything!"

Julio said, "Berta, let's go to the kitchen. Don't worry. Jesus used to multiply food, and He hasn't forgotten how to do that. He is the same. He hasn't changed. So we are going to pray."

They prayed a simple prayer, "Jesus, thank you for the food. Please multiply the food."

At that time, the prayers were very simple and full of faith. So Berta began to serve. One, two, twenty. And the food kept coming. Thirty, forty. And Berta began to cry because she knew she was witnessing a miracle. Everyone ate, and some of them went back for seconds because they were still hungry. And everyone was so happy because the pan remained half full.

Next, Julio said, "Let's have the communion."
They said, "We don't have wine, and everything's closed."
Julio said, "Do we have water?"
"Yes."
"Again, Jesus has not forgotten how to make wine from water," Julio replied.

So they brought him a full cup of water, and the water converted to wine. This was unusual. It was beyond anything we had experienced from Jesus so far. People were crying and praying. It is shocking when Jesus moves and does the unexpected. Your mind doesn't comprehend what is going on. All you know is that you have found the reality and presence of the love of Jesus, that He is the same today as He was in Bible days.

After everybody composed themselves, Berta asked, "Where did you guys get the water?"
They said, "From that faucet."
She said, "That cannot be. That is a dry faucet. There is no water connected to it."
They looked and, sure enough, there was nothing connected to it. It was a dry faucet.

How can you explain that? Moses got water from the rock, and in Bolivia water came from a dry faucet.

God remains the same. His power, His majesty, His mercy are forever.

CHAPTER 4

A CHURCH IS BORN

We read in the first chapters of Acts how the Church was born through the power and guidance of the Holy Spirit. We need to understand that the Holy Spirit alone knows the will of God, and He is the One working every day, 24 hours a day, to prepare and build the Church that is going to be the bride of our Lord Jesus Christ. He promised that His bride would be perfect, without blemish or wrinkle (Ephesians 5:25-27).

How was a church born in Bolivia? As I mentioned before, Bolivia was infamously known as the nightmare of missionaries. In this chapter, we are going to share our experience of how the Holy Spirit brought the Gospel to Bolivia through very young, immature, and unprepared people. Something that we have to remember always is that God does not change and is forever. Jesus is the same. He does not change. In James 1:16 and 17, it is written:

Do not be deceived, my beloved brethren. Every good gift and every perfect gift is from above and comes down from the Father of Lights, with whom there is no variation or shadow of turning.

So God the Father, Jesus Christ, and the Holy Spirit are the same forever. They don't change. Their love, mercy, peace, and joy are the same. Their voices and personalities remain the same. And also, their plans and strategies are the same. The Lord has always used the small, despised, and foolish things of the world to shame the wise. The greatest and most awesome works of God have come from humble beginnings.

Jesus, the King, was born in a manger; Pentecost consisted of a few followers gathered to wait for the promised Holy Spirit in a humble house. God used those 120 faithful ones to transform the entire world with the message of the Gospel, demonstrated in power, signs, and wonders.

God has not changed. He always uses the rejected of the world, the smallest, poorest, and most humble nations. If God chose a simple home to bring power that would transform the world, why would He not use the same tactics, approach, and strategies to deliver His Gospel today?

All revivals are birthed from the will of God, not through the agendas, material means, and charisma of men. By going back to the basics of the Bible and past revivals in history, generations to come can learn from those legacies and gain vision of how God works, and His plans for gathering the nations to Himself before Jesus returns. While God is the ultimate source of creativity and will constantly surprise and delight us with His works and ways, His character and nature remain consistent and unchanging throughout the ages. He may find new people to use to preach His Gospel through signs and wonders of healing, but He never changes. He serves as a loving Father with a desire to heal, restore, and reconcile. That is His nature.

Furthermore, He may use the technology of men to advance the Gospel, but the message of the Gospel remains unchanged. His Word remains unchanging and sharper than a double-edged sword (Hebrews 4:12), serving as our ultimate weapon against Satan's tactics and lies (Ephesians 6:17). We live in a culture of constant change—especially when it comes to standards of living, technology, and science. We are always looking for something new: new cars, new phones, new houses, new clothes, new movies. In our minds, change is good, and we expect the same with God, that He is constantly changing.

I'm always surprised as to how many changes the Church is looking to implement. If there is a conference about change, everyone wants to attend. And everybody gets excited because everyone expects something new.

We try to do everything in new and exciting ways. In churches, we are looking for better sound systems, better seats, better technology, and we are always looking to please the people that come to the church. We do everything possible to entertain and motivate the minds and emotions of people, thinking that God is in that.

This is a big mistake.

The first church was born after Pentecost and met in houses. When the apostles wrote to the church, they addressed the letters to the household where believers met.

In Acts 2:40-47 of the New King James Version, we read:

And with many other words, he (Peter) testified and exhorted them, saying, 'Be saved from this perverse generation.' Then those who gladly received his word were baptized. On that day, about

3,000 souls were added to them. And they continued, steadfastly, in the apostles' doctrine and fellowship, in the breaking of bread and prayers. Then fear came upon every soul, and many wonders and signs were done through the apostles.

Now, all who believed were together and had all things in common and sold their possessions and goods and divided them among all, as anyone had need. So, continuing daily with one accord in the temple and breaking bread from house to house, they ate their food with gladness and simplicity of heart, praising God and having favor with all the people, and the Lord added to the church daily those who were being saved.

The strategy of the Holy Spirit was for the church to begin in houses, and He was the One who was adding the people that were saved. It was work done by the Holy Spirit and not by man. In Bolivia, the salvations happened in the same way. At that time, we did not have a clue what this was all about. We had no knowledge of the Word of God, no plans, and no agendas. The only thing we knew was that Jesus was alive and that the Holy Spirit was walking, talking, and interacting with us every day.

When Julio arrived in Bolivia, he was obedient to the Word of God and to the voice of God that told him to go and preach the gospel to Bolivia. He didn't know all the details. He didn't have a plan. Actually, he didn't have a clue as to how this was going to be accomplished. Julio tried talking to the traditional churches in Bolivia, but he was rejected because they thought that he was a false prophet and exaggerating when he told them that God was going to touch Bolivia.

He didn't know where to go. He prayed, and the Holy Spirit told him, "Go to your friends and share the gospel with them." So he did.

And the Holy Spirit began to touch his friends in a powerful way—so much so that everyone's experiences were so deep and rich because they all had encounters with the Living God. A common denominator was the fact that they knew that Jesus was alive and that the Holy Spirit was the Teacher, Guide, Companion, and Friend (John 14:16). Their eyes were opened, and their lives were totally changed with such a conviction that they were willing to leave everything and give anything to walk with God. They were young and totally surrendered to the Holy Spirit.

The Word began to spread out from friend to friend, from neighbor to neighbor in the streets and the houses of the cities throughout Bolivia. In the beginning, no more than ten people would gather in each house. But the Holy Spirit began to manifest Himself in the midst of these small meetings, and healings and miracles began to take place. Also, all of those who gathered were baptized with the Holy Spirit.

The meetings in houses began to grow in the city. La Paz had close to one million people. It was a big city. But the Holy Spirit began to move everywhere, and these meetings began to increase very rapidly. The Holy Spirit began to add to the ones who were being saved, and the numbers began to grow as people heard and responded to the Gospel. The multiplication began gradually and built up steadily, like a volcano priming for an explosion.

Because of the need, Julio had to send young people two by two to share the Gospel in these houses. These young men and women were newly converted. They didn't have preparation. They didn't have knowledge. But they had faith—simple faith in Jesus. The Holy Spirit began to use them with miracles, healings, and wonders following.

The city of La Paz began to be permeated by the Gospel to the point where everybody began to talk about God, Jesus, and the Holy Spirit. The crowds grew too large for the houses and the city squares, so people began to go to the terraces and then to the coliseums. God began to open doors in high schools, middle schools, and radio stations. We were at the doors of the revival that was promised.

This revival was not about one man, Julio Ruibal, preaching. The Holy Spirit used so many young men and women. At that time, there was not any infrastructure that we could use. The traditional churches were really, really small, and the rest of the churches were Catholic. God was moving, more and more strongly. Every day, hundreds of people began to come to the Lord. In a month's time, there were thousands coming to God every day.

At that time, Julio began to talk about preaching in the stadiums. He said that even the stadiums were going to be too small and they would not hold all the people that the Holy Spirit was going to bring. Julio began to search the Lord in a deeper way—praying and fasting constantly. He was searching for the will of the Holy Spirit and the perfect time and place the Spirit was going to move.

Every time that I travel through Latin America sharing with pastors and churches from many denominations, we usually discuss revival. They always ask, "How are we going to pay for it?" Next, they express their desire to experience a revival.

My response has always been, because of my experience, "You're asking for a revival? You don't know what you are asking for because it's going to cost you everything that you have. It will cost you your time, your plans, and preparation. If you are not totally surrendered to the Holy Spirit, nothing is going to happen."

And to their question about financing, I always answer, "God can and will finance His revival."

And that's exactly what happened in Bolivia.

Julio totally surrendered his life to Jesus and the Holy Spirit. When he first gave his heart and life to Jesus, he went to his room, laid on the floor, raised his hands and said, "Jesus, I don't need anything or anybody because I have You."

That was his heart. He only had one dream—to do the will of God and to be obedient to God.

CHAPTER 5

THE EXPLOSION

In December of '72, during Bolivia's summer, Julio prayed and fasted until he said, "I think it's time for the stadiums."

His deacons, the young leaders, said, "Look, Julio, we're going to need this much money to rent the stadium and to do the promotional announcements."

Julio had decided to go back to the United States, and he told them, "Look, I'm going to go to the United States because the church there is very generous, and they will help us to raise the money for the stadiums."

Everybody was very happy.

Julio left, and when he arrived in the United States, he was very excited as to how God was going to provide the money. So he went from church to church, and the response was always, "Julio, we are so proud of you. We are so happy that you are going to be preaching the gospel in Bolivia. We will be praying for you."

But they didn't give him a dime or a penny.

Julio became frustrated because he couldn't raise the money that he needed. He decided to fast and to search for God some more.

Jesus told him, "Julio, go back to Bolivia because I'm going to do it My way."

In Bolivia, everybody was expecting him with much excitement. As soon as he got off the plane, they asked him, "Julio, did you get the money?"

He said, "No, but don't worry. Jesus said that He will do it His way. Just as He promised. *Así lo prometió.*" So they continued with the work.

By then, almost everyone in La Paz was talking about how Jesus was doing miracles again, that He was alive, and there was a big commotion all over the city. Many people were being healed, and miracles were taking place, and wonders were happening throughout the city.

One day, David Farah, Director of the Wycliffe Bible Translators in Bolivia, invited Julio to pray for a young man. His name was Guido Gutiérrez. He was part of President General Hugo Banzer Suarez's cabinet. He had been in an accident and was paralyzed from the waist down.

Julio told David, "Look, I don't want you to think that I am a healer or a magician. I am mostly interested in a soul being saved. I will go to pray first for him to be saved."

Julio came to the hospital and said to Gutiérrez, "I think your soul is more important than your body because it is better to live eternally as a paralytic than to suffer eternal punishment for your sins. To me, salvation is the most important miracle in the life of a human being."

Gutiérrez repented and gave his life to Jesus.

While he was praying, someone noticed his toes twitching. When he looked down at his feet, they began to move. He began to move his legs, and a commotion erupted in that hospital—so much so that everyone began to scream.

He began to cry, "I'm healed! I'm healed!"

It was just like in the times of Jesus. Julio had to get away because a mob of sick people began chasing after him, looking for healing.

Julio was 19 years old, and every member of his leadership was around that age. Since they were so young, they enjoyed pulling pranks amongst themselves, and they were always laughing and playing. That was the atmosphere of their fellowship.

One day, they knocked on Julio's door and said, "Julio, the President wants to talk to you."

Since Julio thought his friends were pulling another prank, he opened the door and grew very angry. He said, "Guys, I'm very busy with meetings. Why did you wake me up?"

They said, "For real, he wants to talk to you!"

Outside, Julio stepped into a government vehicle and found himself in the presence of the President of Bolivia, General Hugo Banzer Suarez.

The President said to Julio, "I am so grateful for what you have done for my friend. What do you need?"

Julio said, "I don't need anything. But I see you are tired with all the responsibilities of leading this nation on your shoulders. I think, Mr. President, you need Jesus."

And so the president and his wife got on their knees and received Jesus as their savior.

He stood up and said, "Julio, I want to help you. What do you really need?"

Julio said, "Mr. President, I don't need anything. But I think this nation needs to hear the gospel."

The President asked, "How can I help?"

Julio said, "We need the stadiums, and we need radios and television and transportation."

At that, the President said, "It's done."

In a single day, Jesus, who has not changed, through the Holy Spirit, opened the door and provided Julio with the means to preach the gospel.

> *So he (President Banzer) opened up Bolivia for the preaching of the Gospel. The president gave us prime time on television and radio. He had his assistants call the mayors of every major city and arrange invitations for us to come and preach* (Ruibal 25).

Así lo prometió—as He promised.

The revival in Bolivia did not cost a penny. It was paid for when Jesus died on the cross. *Everything* was paid at the cross. With God's help, the revival explosion soon took place. Radio announcements and television advertisements began for the meetings at the stadium in La Paz. The first meeting was to be Sunday, the 14th of January, 1973.

Many radio stations began to interview Julio because of his extraordinarily charismatic qualities as a leader and the wonders and healings that were done through his hands. There was such a spiritual atmosphere in La Paz, along with a curiosity and hunger for the things of God, that people began to gather at the stadium the night before just to make sure they found a seat.

The next morning, the multitudes began to enter the stadium, which had a capacity of 25,000 people. The stadium reached full capacity, as well as the soccer field, where a platform was erected for Julio to stand on and preach the gospel. Around the platform, there were many reporters, both local and international, from different newspapers, TV and radio stations to record the event. People brought sick people and relatives, and they were placed inside the soccer field. People from every strata of society attended the meeting—rich, poor, educated, uneducated, male, female, children, adults.

One reporter said, "I didn't know that there were so many sick people in Bolivia," due to the numbers of people with different ailments. The sense of expectation began to grow. People that arrived the night before had to sleep on the ground inside of the stadium. This stadium did not have a roof covering. On that particular night, it rained. But it rained around the stadium, not in the stadium. It was like someone put a giant umbrella over the people, and no one got wet. This miracle was noted by everybody, even the reporters. They could see that God was there and that this was not a normal meeting.

On the day of the meeting, supernatural peace invaded the atmosphere and created deep reverence for the presence of God. Julio appeared. He was dressed in a white suit that God told him to wear. He started with a simple prayer, and his sermon was not as sophisticated as many thought it would be. He began to talk about the love of God, His power as King of kings and His infinite capacity to forgive people.

He said, "The love of Christ is forever and has not changed. Regardless of the passing of time or regardless of what science has said, He is the same Jesus, just as He was walking 2,000 years ago. We, brothers, with our attitude and apathy, with our lack of trust and with our hearts that are so hard, crucify Jesus on the cross every day." He spoke to the sick people, many of whom were crying.

He said, "God loves you, and He is looking at you. He has compassion on you. He suffers to feel your pain, your illness."

That was the message, mainly. After that, he prayed and asked everyone to pray. While they were praying, the miracles began to happen. Paralytics, the blind, the deaf, and mute were all healed. It was like a deluge of healings and miracles that were taking place so quickly that no one could keep up with them. People were crying and screaming everywhere.

The river of the Holy Spirit was filling everything and touching everybody. In the crowd, people were having real encounters with the love, peace, and grace of our Lord Jesus.

> Healings took place in such proportions that dozens of crutches, orthopedic gadgets, canes, and braces were collected after every meeting. Generals were healed as well as poor peasants. The whole nation heard and millions throughout the nations of the world read the reports of what God was doing in this small country in the middle of South America (Ruibal 25).

People began to praise God and to pray without being prompted. Nobody put hands on the sick people. Nobody told people to repent. There was not a human plan. There was not an agenda. Everything began to happen spontaneously, and the name of Jesus was glorified.

The Holy Spirit was free to touch the deepest heart of every person, bringing them to repentance from their sinful lives and also to the revelation of the fact that Jesus Christ is the Son of God who was crucified for their sins, rose from the dead and is alive. Truly, nobody could explain what happened. The reporters couldn't understand what was happening, nor could they believe what their eyes were seeing.

Twenty-five thousand people gave their lives to Christ in less than an hour and a half. And that was only the first meeting.

The gospel had finally come to Bolivia, and the words of Jesus were fulfilled: "I will do it My way." And that's the only way He does things.

From then on, the front page of every newspaper in La Paz read, "Miracles are happening in La Paz, Bolivia." The demand for newspapers was so high that citizens struggled to find a single newspaper. The radios were talking; television was talking. Everyone was talking about Jesus.

> *The press came from all over the world. TV reporters from Mexico, Argentina, and the USA. NBC, UP, UPI, Reuters, and the British press came to film what was taking place (Ruibal 27).*

The next stadium meeting took place on January 20 with the same results, same intensity, same miracles, same reactions. Truly, people began to understand that only God could have done such a thing. The last meeting took place the next day, Sunday the 21st.

With their expectations and curiosity fulfilled, more people began to come.

The third meeting was the largest stadium meeting held in La Paz. Hernando Siles Stadium held 25,000 people inside and could not contain the additional 40,000+ people outside who gathered to hear the Gospel preached. Everybody was in shock. They could not understand how a 19-year-old kid with a Bible in his hand could fill the stadium in such a way. Before, not even the Brazilian team with Pele, the world's best soccer player at the time, could fill that stadium. For God, nothing is impossible.

People from all over arrived the day before and waited throughout the night, so the leaders in charge of that particular meeting called Julio around midnight and told him, "Look, there are 20,000 or more people waiting outside."

"Let them in," said Julio.

They also noted that by early morning, the stadium was already full and many more tens of thousands were gathering outside. The leadership thought, "We need to place speakers outside the stadium so people can hear Julio preaching."

They went and talked to the administrator of the stadium and asked him if he had speakers. They found two old, big, and heavy speakers and placed them outside the stadium. But there was a problem. They needed enough cables to hook the speakers to the power source and the microphones on stage. Then they realized that they did not have enough cables. They left the speakers outside the stadium unplugged, without any connection to a power source.

Julio, as always, asked the Holy Spirit what to wear. That particular day, the Holy Spirit told him not to wear his white suit. He was just obedient. So when the time came to go to the stadium, everything was blocked. Julio had to walk into the stadium, pretending to be a reporter. People didn't recognize him because they were looking for someone dressed in a white suit, so he was able to get in and start preaching. He then realized that the people outside were even more in number than the people inside, and everyone wanted to hear the Word of God.

He said to his friends, "I'm going to go to the roof, and I'm going to preach again to them." So Julio preached twice that day, once inside and then outside the stadium.

He climbed to the top of the roof of the stadium, facing the crowds, and everyone was afraid he was going to fall. Two of his friends went with him to hold up his legs, and Julio began to preach.

He raised his arms, and it was like a river was flowing through the people because they began to sway back and forth as he preached. Something miraculous happened. The two speakers that were left unplugged with no connection to power started working perfectly. People could hear Julio's voice clearly in every direction. The display of God's power, grace, and love meeting the peoples' hunger in such a miraculous way was indescribable.

CHAPTER 6

ALL-CONSUMING FIRE

The fire began to burn in Bolivia. The rest of the main cities in Bolivia began to invite Julio to preach the gospel.

In only two weeks, the Bible Society sold 33,000 Bibles, New Testaments, and gospel portions. They exhausted their stock and in the emergency had to fly in shipments of Bibles from Argentina, Paraguay, and Peru. Bolivia had become the center of world-renowned religious activity. The power of God was manifested with awesome works (Ruibal 27).

Everybody wanted to read the Bible. Everyone was hungry. And everyone was conscious that Jesus is alive.

Santa Cruz

So, like a spiritual atomic explosion, news about the revival and the first meetings in La Paz spread everywhere. My fellow Bolivian citizens began to talk about the fact that Jesus is alive and that miracles and healings and wonders were taking place again. People began to understand and see that Jesus is the same, and His love, mercy, power, and healing abilities have not changed in 2,000 years.

Everybody was talking about Jesus. All levels of society, from regular people to politicians to religious leaders, were affected by the revival. Every other big city in Bolivia wanted to experience revival, the power of the Gospel. Julio was invited to preach in Santa Cruz, which, at that time, was the second largest city in Bolivia. And so, it was announced through various media that Julio would arrive in Santa Cruz on Saturday, January 27, 1973.

He arrived at the El Trompillo airport around 10:30 a.m. Close to 9,000 people were already at the airport awaiting his arrival. In the meeting, Julio spoke about the love of Jesus and His power. Although no healings or miracles took place at that time, the Holy Spirit began to move, and people began to cry.

Later that day, Julio arrived at the monument of Cristo Redentor where more than 40,000 people were waiting to hear him preach. That day something unusual happened that everyone noticed, including reporters from different countries. Santa Cruz is located in the tropics and experiences very high temperatures. The particular afternoon that Julio spoke, the sky was blue with no clouds to be seen, and it was very hot. In spite of the heat, many sick people in wheelchairs, on crutches, the blind and deaf, children, women, men, old, young, were waiting to hear the Gospel.

When Julio stood up on top of the platform some people had built above the famous monument, he waved to the crowds of people. Suddenly, a strong wind swept across the crowd and pushed a cloud that covered everyone like an umbrella. The cloud did not move until the meeting was over.

> *The wind blows where it wishes, and you hear its sound,*
> *but you do not know where it comes from or where it goes.*
> *So it is with everyone who is born of the Spirit.*
>
> John 3:8

Once again, God was showing Himself to the people. Julio spoke about the love of God, about His unchanging power and mercy. He loved the people so much that He made sure they were cool and comfortable during the meeting. As Julio preached, miracles and healings began to take place. People using wheelchairs began to walk. People that had been deaf their entire lives began to hear. The blind began to see. The explosion of miracles and healings caught everyone by surprise. People could not believe what they were hearing and seeing.

Everybody was crying. They were being confronted by the fact that Jesus died on the cross for their sins, was resurrected, and is really and truly alive. After a simple message, Julio concluded by asking everyone to lift their hands and pray. It was a time of solemn reverence before God. People of all ages began to talk and pray to Jesus. Julio left, but God continued to perform miracles. The Holy Spirit was busy healing, touching, comforting—doing the things that He is an expert at doing.

The next day, on the Sunday morning of January 28, Julio spoke again.

Julio said that we should not seek the pleasures of this world that are so superficial. Instead, true Christians have something far better.

Do not lay up for yourselves treasures on earth, where moth and rust destroy and where thieves break in and steal, but lay up for yourselves treasures in heaven, where neither moth nor rust destroys and where thieves do not break in and steal.
Matthew 6:19-21

True Christians have the fruit of the Spirit, which is more valuable.

But the fruit of the Holy Spirit is love, joy, peace, patience, kindness, goodness, faithfulness, gentleness, self-control; against such things, there is no law.
Galatians 5:22-23

Again, his message was very simple. As he spoke, an explosion of miracles and healings broke out with greater intensity than the day before. This time, many more than 40,000 people attended and listened to the Gospel. This was unprecedented in Bolivia, that so many people were coming together to seek God. Everybody was in shock once again. They could not believe what they were witnessing. Everybody was talking about Jesus. Even communities outside of Santa Cruz were talking about Jesus.

And so, the next day, Monday, the mayor of the small city of Portachuelo sent a message to Julio and told him that people were waiting for him to come and speak. Thousands had already congregated in the main Plaza. The only problem was that the city was far away, and they didn't have an airport.

So Julio did the next best thing that he could—he flew in an airplane around the Plaza and began to pray for the people below. Suddenly, again, an explosion of miracles and healings took place. People began to weep and wave their handkerchiefs to him. It was like a scene from the Book of Acts of the Apostles, straight out of the Bible, when Peter's shadow healed the sick.

As a result of the apostles' work, sick people were brought out into the streets on beds and mats so that Peter's shadow might fall across some of them as he went by.

Acts 5:15 NLT

This time, it was the shadow of a plane—the same Holy Spirit, just another method. God is very, very creative, and nothing is impossible for Him. When He moves, He is like an avalanche—nothing can stop Him.

Cochabamba

From Santa Cruz, Julio flew to Cochabamba, which at that time was the third largest city in Bolivia. Again, everybody was awaiting his arrival with high expectations. The only problem was where to hold the meetings because the stadiums were too small to contain such a multitude of people. So they chose La Coronilla for the meeting place, which is a hill in the city of Cochabamba.

The first meeting took place on Saturday, February 3 and began around 4 p.m. Again, the meeting place was filled with people in great expectation. Many of them had spent all day waiting for Julio. More than 60,000 people gathered, including the sick, the lame, the deaf, and the blind. People from hospitals began to arrive at the site in ambulances. All waited for a touch from God.

Again, the weather was very hot, as the meeting took place in summer, but nobody cared about the heat. Everybody wanted to have an encounter with Jesus. Julio delivered yet another simple message.

He said, "Jesus is the Way, the Truth, and the Life. No one comes to the Father except through Him, and the Holy Spirit is the One that does the healings and miracles."

He exhorted people to love each other because God is love (1 John 4:7-8). He called for them to repent. He prayed for the Holy Spirit to heal and to touch and to take away pain and sickness. Like in Santa Cruz, the gospel was preached through miracles and healings. Everybody was crying. And everybody began to pray and open their hearts to Jesus. There were so many miracles that all the wheelchairs, crutches, orthopedic braces, glasses, and hearing aids that were no longer needed filled up an entire semi-truck.

People began to scream, wail, and express many different emotions because of the miracles they witnessed. Everybody began to try to reason how these things could take place. They were facing the reality of a Living Jesus Christ, and their natural minds could not comprehend it. But the facts were there and could not be denied.

Jesus was speaking once again through Julio to multitudes on a hill.

Something interesting happened at this particular meeting. The sound equipment was not good. And yet, everybody could hear Julio's voice as though he were speaking directly into their ears. From the top to the bottom of the hill, and for perhaps four to five blocks beyond, every person in the crowd could hear him, though he spoke in a soft tone, not shouting.

Later on, I met people who told me they were close to 50 or 60 blocks away and could only see Julio as a small dot. And yet, they could clearly hear his voice and decided to give their lives to Christ.

I think that Jesus did something similar on the Mount when He spoke to multitudes without any sound equipment. The sound equipment that the Holy Spirit uses is more sophisticated than anything since there is no distance for Him. The Gospel of Jesus Christ was preached and demonstrated with power. The signs and wonders beautifully demonstrated the love, mercy, grace, and power of our Lord Jesus Christ.

Jesus Christ was the main theme of conversations on the radio, TV, in houses, hospitals, banks—everywhere. Literally, Bolivia became a platform for the display of His power and love.

The second meeting took place the next day. People spent the night before waiting for the meeting. Many more people came to this meeting. The place was so packed that people stood on the hill and all the way down through the streets and avenues. Perhaps more than 100,000 people attended the second meeting. People came from everywhere, including different countries in and around South America. The meeting started at 10:00 a.m. It was a peaceful morning, and everybody was simply whispering. Nobody was talking loudly.

There was a particular weight of reverence in that place. People could sense that Someone Holy was there. Julio began with a simple message exhorting people to follow God and to seek Him through His Son Jesus

Christ. He never discussed denomination. The only One he ever talked about was Jesus, and that through Him was Life.

Most of these people had heard about Jesus through the Catholic Church but had never had an encounter with Jesus Himself. These meetings were not about religion but an encounter with the love of God. Many people in other cities were following these meetings through radio and television. Eventually, the message of the Gospel reached every part of Bolivia. By now, millions of people in Bolivia had heard the Gospel and given their lives to Jesus. Paul said:

> *When I came to you, brothers, I did not come with eloquence or superior wisdom ... My message and my preaching were not with wise and persuasive words, but with demonstration of great spiritual power so your faith would not rest on men's wisdom but on God's power.*
> 1 Corinthians 2:1-5 NIV

> As God moved in Bolivia, the country was transformed. For the first time in its history, there was stability with a president that stayed in power for seven years. The nation experienced its first economic boom. History had been changed!
>
> But Bolivia was not transformed by my eloquence or my persuasive words but rather by the Spirit of God. Sixty percent of the population were peasants or natives. Many of them could not understand me clearly. Yet, even though they didn't understand my words, they believed because they saw the power of God that speaks to every heart and reaches down to the deepest needs of men (Ruibal 30).

Like at the other meetings, the display of the power and love of God was awesome, confirming with miracles the preaching of the Gospel. God was totally visiting Bolivia. For the first time, a whole nation was touched by God. The revival was not for one city or one church, but for an entire nation.

> A New Tribes' missionary told me five years later that the magnitude of the visitation of God in Bolivia during that time was so great that in the middle of the jungles, where only indigenous

tribes and colonists lived, they found groups of people from the interior gathered together. The missionary asked why they were there, and they responded, "We are waiting for someone to tell us about God." They had no knowledge of the crusades; it was a totally supernatural work of the Holy Spirit (Ruibal 27).

Oruro: A Hard Lesson to Learn

Apart from Me, you can do nothing.

John 15:5

For am I now seeking the approval of man, or of God? Or am I trying to please man? If I were still trying to please man, I would not be a servant of Christ.

Galatians 1:10

And Samuel said, "Has the LORD as great delight in burnt offerings and sacrifices, as in obeying the voice of the LORD? Behold, to obey is better than sacrifice, and to listen than the fat of rams."

1 Samuel 15:22

Julio was totally dependent on the Holy Spirit. He would pray until a place, a date, and a time were given by the Holy Spirit to have a meeting. This particular time, Julio was in La Paz, and somebody came and said, "Julio, do you know that you are preaching this afternoon in Oruro?"

Julio said, "I'm not because I don't have a date yet."

And they said, "Julio, look. You are on the first page of the newspaper. And they are saying that people are already waiting for you in a stadium in Oruro. You have to go. You don't have any other choice."

Oruro is a city in Bolivia that is famous for open Satanic worship. Since Oruro is a mining city, many citizens rely on demonic assistance to locate lucrative veins within the walls of the caves they mine in. They offer sacrifices to Satan and his demons in exchange for knowledge in navigating the underground tunnels for gems and riches. Deep within the mines, many statues and idols of demonic images can be found covered in gifts of gratitude and supplication. Although this city boasts much material wealth, even today, Oruro suffers from much chaos, disorder, and destruction due to demonic oppression.

Every year, millions of tourists from around the world travel to Bolivia for Carnaval de Oruro, the annual musical celebration that has been taking place for over 200 years. The highlight of this festival is Oruro Diablada—the dance of the devils, which pays homage to the gods of the mines. The miners are indebted to Satan. Many hand over their souls in exchange for the worldly riches he offers them, just as he tempted Jesus with money and power in the desert (Matthew 4:8-9). Many Christians, especially Westerners, doubt Satan's power and influence over this world—many even doubt his existence.

> "The first trick of the devil is to make you think there is no devil."
>
> —Julio Ruibal

We need to remember that Jesus was tempted by Satan himself and a large portion of His recorded miracles involved delivering people who suffered demonic torment of various kinds. While we are not to focus our energy on Satan or his schemes, Jesus commanded us to use our God-given authority over Satan and his demons.

> *He said to them, "I saw Satan fall like lightning from heaven. Behold, I have given you authority to tread on serpents and scorpions, and over all the power of the enemy, and nothing shall hurt you. Nevertheless, do not rejoice that the spirits submit to you, but rejoice that your names are written in heaven."*
>
> Luke 10:18-20

> *Heal the sick, raise the dead, cleanse those who have leprosy, drive out demons. Freely you have received; freely give.*
>
> Matthew 10:8 NIV

So, Julio went to Oruro, the mine-centered city not far from La Paz. When he arrived, the stadium was full. This time, though, there was no sense of order. People were not behaving the way they behaved in the rest of the cities in Bolivia when Julio preached. Everybody there wanted to touch Julio because they thought he was the one healing people.

Julio became agitated and actually angry. He began to tell them, "I'm not a healer. Jesus is the One who heals."

But people wouldn't hear that. They began to scream, whistle, and boo. Julio was so angry, he took his shoes off and began to clap them together and shake the dust off of his feet in a curse. He promptly left and did not speak a single word.

> *As you enter the house, greet it. And if the house is worthy, let your peace come upon it, but if it is not worthy, let your peace return to you. And if anyone will not receive you or listen to your words, shake off the dust from your feet when you leave that house or town. Truly, I say to you; it will be more bearable on the day of judgment for the land of Sodom and Gomorrah than for that town.*
>
> Matthew 10:12-15

> *And when the Gentiles heard this, they began rejoicing and glorifying the word of the Lord, and as many as were appointed to eternal life believed. And the word of the Lord was spreading throughout the whole region. But the Jews incited the devout women of high standing and the leading men of the city, stirred up persecution against Paul and Barnabas, and drove them out of their district. But they shook off the dust from their feet against them and went to Iconium.*
>
> Acts 13:48-51

Nothing happened. There were no signs, healings, or wonders. Julio was nowhere to be found.

He went straight to the mountains to cry. As he was crying, the Holy Spirit revealed a valuable lesson to him: "The enemy is going to try to stop you. And if he can't, he will push you so you won't be on the divine appointment time for that particular place." Julio was learning again how important it was to understand the time and place that God has for everything. That was a crucial lesson we all learned from the Holy Spirit.

From the moment Julio shook the dust off his feet, the city of Oruro was under a curse from God. The atmosphere, already oppressive due to open idolatry, became so sterile and dead that it was impossible even to pray, much less preach the gospel.

CHAPTER 7

A SPIRIT-BORN CHURCH

When I travel around Latin America and meet with pastors and leaders from different ministries and denominations, I have noticed a deep longing for revival.

I tell them, "You guys don't know what you are asking or wishing for. The price is high because it will literally take all your life and everything you have. When revival comes, there is no time for anything else. You have to sacrifice everything for the good of the Gospel."

During the revival in Bolivia, we were not prepared. We didn't have a clue what to expect. The revival was so large and so intense that we did not have the infrastructure to hold the multitudes of people. We didn't have churches or places in which to meet. All the very small traditional churches that did exist were filled to capacity. We didn't have Bible colleges to absorb and prepare the people that wanted to serve God. We didn't have teachers, leaders, or preachers. We didn't have anything. I guess this was a blessing in disguise. Because we had the most important Person in the world, the Holy Spirit, He became our Teacher, our Guide, our Counselor, our Friend—everything to us. Looking back, I think both being unprepared and being prepared have their own pitfalls.

We were totally unprepared. We didn't have any theological understanding of the Word, and we were clueless as to how to proceed. To me, this was not just a handicap but a blessing in many ways. I could not lean on my own knowledge, experience, or strength. I had to rely completely on the guidance of the Holy Spirit, His teachings, and His anointing. I had to rely 100% on God. He was my Light, my Strength, my Life—He was my everything.

Having said that, looking back 45 years, I think we do need some type of preparation today so that we don't make the same mistakes that were made and gain a clearer understanding of what God wants to do today through the scriptures. To me, it is about having a balanced approach to this issue. My advice to the new generation in the light of revival is going to be this: Prepare as much as you can, but never rely on your own preparation or strength—rely on the Holy Spirit.

When you have that balance of the Spirit and the Word, you are in the perfect place for revival to happen.

CHAPTER 8

THE SIMPLE GOSPEL

Because we were not exposed to any teachings of men, we only drank from the pure, unadulterated milk of the Word as spiritual babies (1 Peter 2:2). We didn't have any preconceptions of denominations or theologies. We thought that it was the same everywhere else. We became more than friends. We considered each other brothers and sisters. We became a family. To us, everybody was the same. Our only emphasis was on the fact that Jesus was alive, the Church was one, and we were supposed to love each other.

Brothers and sisters continued to meet in houses and parks. Thousands and thousands of small groups began to spring up throughout the cities. God poured a supernatural love in our hearts—love that endured for decades. Right now, I still love my brothers and sisters in Bolivia, although I live in another country. Every time that we see each other, we still have the same love for each other. To me, this is remarkable because, through time, people change—everything changes. But the love of God that was poured into our hearts by the Holy Spirit remains the same (Romans 5:5).

Most of us were students who didn't have much money. We were very young, and some of us left everything just to preach the Gospel. In the beginning, we spent hours upon hours praying and worshipping together and constantly searching for the tangible presence of the Holy Spirit. We needed to feel His presence in our lives.

I think one of the most important tasks that the Holy Spirit has is to unite the Church. Every believer who believes and receives the baptism of the Holy Spirit should work, pray, and seek the unity of the Church, because that is what the Holy Spirit does. One day, the Holy Spirit is going to have one Church without blemish, and in all power, like a Bride, waiting for the Lord Jesus (Ephesians 5:27). I know that He will accomplish this, and He will do a perfect job. With the Holy Spirit, everything is about perfection. He is perfect, and His works are perfect in every way.

You, therefore, must be perfect, as your heavenly Father is perfect.
Matthew 5:48 NIV

CHAPTER 9

THOUSAND-YEAR DAYS ('71 - '73)

But do not overlook this one fact, beloved, that with the Lord one day is as a thousand years and a thousand years as one day.
                                                                2 Peter 3:8

We need to remember that Jesus had an active ministry for only three years. With higher heavenly activity, time passes in an accelerated way on earth. When heaven pours out a river of supernatural power, time on earth begins to align with heaven. So much can happen in a short time. People's hearts were changed very fast, almost instantaneously. God was able to do in hours what would normally take years in counseling or ministry.

For example, my wife, Laura, had a friend who had experienced deep childhood trauma. When she encountered Christ, the Holy Spirit healed her heart so deeply that, within one month, she was completely free from all of the painful emotional and physical trauma of her past.

It has taken me 45 years to understand these things. That is why I understand why John wrote:

If I were to write everything that Jesus did, I suppose that the world itself could not contain the books that would be written.
                                                                John 21:25

What led me to this understanding was the idea that Jesus' ministry was really like a large, rushing river, where millions of gallons of water passed through in a short time.

On the last day of the feast, the great day, Jesus stood up and cried out, "If anyone thirsts, let him come to me and drink. Whoever believes in me, as the Scripture has said, 'Out of his heart will flow rivers of living water.'"
                                                                John 7:37-38

So it was with the revival. If we were to chronicle everything that God did, it would take years and many books. Every day, the Holy Spirit was doing perhaps a million things at once that would take ten natural years to understand or accomplish. The heavenly activity was so accelerated it would be almost impossible to describe in human terms. When revival comes, and the Holy Spirit moves, you enter into a supernatural zone where everything happens outside of time because you move into eternity.

The Church was born in a little over a year because of the great numbers saved. We were born into the ministry almost instantly. Young people began to minister and preach 10 or 15 days after receiving Christ. It was like you gave your life to Christ, got baptized in water, received the baptism of the Holy Spirit, and you became a minister. That happened to so many young men and women. It happened the same way for me.

After I gave my life to Christ, I received the baptism of the Holy Spirit. One night while I was praying, I heard a voice, perhaps two weeks after I was born again. Nobody told me that God spoke. So when I heard this voice, I turned around and looked to see who was talking to me. But everybody was praying. We were young, and we used to play around a lot and just trick each other. So I thought that someone was trying to trick me.

Again I heard, "Fernando." I turned around to see who was trying to trick me.

For a third time, I heard, "Fernando, go and preach my gospel in Oruro."

I was surprised and shocked that God was talking to me.

I went to see my leader, who was three months older than me. I said, "God told me—"

He stopped me right away. He said, "You don't say anything. If He told you something, He's going to tell me the same thing. I'm going to go ask Him."

He went to a corner in the room and began to talk.

I was looking at him, and he was talking to the air. And I was looking at him and thinking, "Who is he talking to?"

It was like he was having a conversation with someone. That looked strange to me. I didn't know these things. I was just a young Catholic with no clue who God was.

He came back to me and said, "Fernando, God told me that you have to go to Oruro to preach the Gospel."

I was surprised and in shock. I thought, "How did he know?" not realizing that God was speaking to him too.

As we were talking, someone else came and said to my leader, "This guy has to go to Oruro to preach the gospel."

That was my introduction to the fact that God continues to speak to His people and that He confirms the words He speaks through believers that make up His Body (2 Corinthians 13:1).

An example of God speaking to a person through His Holy Spirit can be found in 1 Samuel 3:1-10:

Now the boy Samuel was ministering to the Lord in the presence of Eli. And the word of the Lord was rare in those days; there was no frequent vision. At that time, Eli, whose eyesight had begun to grow dim so that he could not see, was lying down in his own place. The lamp of God had not yet gone out, and Samuel was lying down in the temple of the Lord, where the ark of God was.

Then the Lord called Samuel, and he said, "Here I am!" and ran to Eli and said, "Here I am, for you called me." But he said, "I did not call; lie down again." So he went and lay down. And the Lord called again, "Samuel!" and Samuel arose and went to Eli and said, "Here I am, for you called me." But he said, "I did not call, my son; lie down again."

Now Samuel did not yet know the Lord, and the word of the Lord had not yet been revealed to him. And the Lord called Samuel again the third time. And he arose and went to Eli and said, "Here I am, for you called me."

Then Eli perceived that the Lord was calling the boy. Therefore Eli said to Samuel, "Go, lie down, and if he calls you, you shall say, 'Speak, Lord, for your servant hears.'" So Samuel went and lay down in his place. And the Lord came and stood, calling as at other times, "Samuel! Samuel!" And Samuel said, "Speak, for your servant hears."

My problem was that I was a new believer. I had my Bible, and I was just beginning to read Matthew, the first book of the Gospels.

I said to my leader, "I don't know what to preach or what to talk about. I'm so new."

My leader looked at me and said, "Fernando, just open your mouth, and God will fill it."

Well, after seeing so many miracles and healings and then hearing the voice of God, I believed him.

I went to Oruro with a few other brothers.

Obviously, Oruro was in much need of the saving grace of the Gospel of Jesus Christ after the situation that had happened with Julio.

When we arrived, we came to a house that was packed full. Everyone was expecting us. Everyone wanted to meet Jesus and know about Him. Everybody was so hungry for the Word of God.

I stood up, and I opened my mouth. I was just trying to be obedient. To my surprise, nothing came out from my mouth.

Everybody was looking at me like I was crazy, standing with my mouth open. People stood in silence, looking at me.

I began to think, "What am I going to do? I'm in trouble now. Nothing is coming out of my mouth." I was so nervous I began to sweat.

Suddenly, I began to speak. But I was speaking things that I didn't know. It was like someone took my mouth and was using it to speak through me. It is a very, very funny feeling because you are the first to learn what you are saying. I spoke for 45 minutes, and everybody was so happy and so blessed. In that particular meeting, there was a brother from Chile, who came because he heard about the revival. He was a mature Christian, having walked with God for seven or eight years, and he knew the Bible very well.

After the meeting, he asked me, "Fernando, do you know what happened to you?"

I said, "No."

"Do you know what you talked about?"

"No, it was all new to me."

He said, "Fernando, you were quoting Bible verses over and over and over."

I just couldn't believe it. He showed me the Bible verses I had quoted, and I could remember them coming from my mouth. And so we continued to trust and depend wholly on the Holy Spirit because He was with us constantly.

Later on, I read this verse in the Psalms:

Open your mouth wide, and I will fill it.

Psalm 81:10

I don't think my leader knew this verse at that time. Again, the Holy Spirit used his mouth to quote a verse from the Bible, so I could be obedient. That was my first lesson from the Holy Spirit, and now, 44 years later, He still doesn't allow me to prepare any sermon. I just have to open my mouth, and He is so faithful and always fills it with His Word. I think that this experience was shared by other people that were in leadership at that time. Trusting and depending upon the Holy Spirit was vital for us.

As Paul wrote to the Corinthians:

"And we will be ready to punish every act of disobedience once your obedience is complete.

2 Corinthians 10:6

> Our spiritual authority is directly proportional to our obedience to God. If we have 50% obedience, we will only exercise 50% of his authority. If our obedience is complete (that simply means we are walking in light and there is no conscious rebellious attitude in us), then His ministry to us will come in full measure (Ruibal 151).

About 30 years later, while I was praying, the Holy Spirit reminded me that the curse was still over Oruro and that I needed to go back there to break it. Breaking the curse would have been Julio's responsibility, but he was dead by that time.

So I went from the United States all the way to Oruro for this particular mission. And we found the remnants of a very small group that was still meeting there. I saw these people for the first time in 30 years, and they recognized me. I shared with them about the particular prophetic act Julio had performed and that God had sent me to cancel it. I asked them for forgiveness and canceled the curse. The effect was immediate.

The presence of the Holy Spirit was so strong that we literally had to hold onto one another with all our strength because He came like waves in a river. We had to hold on tightly in order not to fall under the weight of His power. I was surprised. The next day, one sister shared her testimony. She said, "Fernando, this is the first time in 30 years that I was able to pray through the night without any problems. Before it was as if the ceiling was made out of metal, and my prayers couldn't go through."

The lesson that I learned was that, especially for people that are preachers and pastors who have higher authority in the Lord, we have to be very careful when it comes to prophetic actions such as these. Sometimes we don't understand the consequences of our words that carry a lot of power in the spiritual realm. Julio had remembered the scriptures about Jesus cursing cities who rejected Him and His disciples (Matthew 10:11-15). He had cursed Oruro out of his own anger—a rash response. Only after he met with God in prayer did he understand the weight of his curse. He carried so much anointing and power that he did not understand that we need to be very careful to seek God before speaking a curse or a blessing. It is better to bless than to curse (Romans 12:14).

CHAPTER 10

WARNINGS

After his last meeting in January 1973, Julio left Bolivia to answer God's call to preach to the rest of South America, and he did not return until December of that year. Meanwhile, meetings continued to take place in houses, plazas—wherever people could find space.

During this time, the Holy Spirit gave us two warnings:

1. Never try to structure His work.
2. Be aware of false doctrines that were about to come from the North.

In the midst of great revival and works of the Spirit, little by little, pride, arrogance, and selfishness began to creep into the hearts of the believers. We began to think that we were the only ones that had the Truth and that we had the monopoly of the Holy Spirit. With that, we began to criticize the traditional denominations and look down on everybody else. It was difficult to receive correction from anyone. Little by little, the Holy Spirit began to step aside. Many believers began to fall back into worldly ways. It was difficult to see so many people that had been touched by God going back to their old ways.

Due to the warning about false doctrines, we began to suspect anything and everybody. Many ministries from the United States came to Bolivia trying to help us. We closed our hearts and minds to them and their efforts. We thought we would stay safe in this way.

Regarding the first warning about structuring the work of the Holy Spirit, in the beginning, the meetings were free of any plans or schedules. We knew the minute the meeting would start, but we never knew when it would end. The Holy Spirit was free to do whatever He saw necessary to do because He is the only One that knows the hearts of the believers. With that in mind, we tried not to interfere with Him. The only desire in our hearts was to be able to enjoy His presence, and the meetings were all about looking and searching for the manifest presence of the Holy Spirit. In that realm and that atmosphere, time is of no importance because we enter into eternity, which is the realm in which God lives, outside of time and space.

Our meetings could last hours and hours, and we wouldn't notice because the time had passed so quickly. We were just in awe of His love, His grace, His presence. We didn't prepare any messages, and we didn't schedule speakers. The Holy Spirit would choose whom to use and what to share. The meetings were not always the same because there was freedom in every way. Our aim was to satisfy the Lord, to glorify Him, and to be totally obedient to Him. That lack of structure and our pure intentions also began to change with the passing of time.

Leaders began to establish a schedule based on man's needs, rather than the Holy Spirit's leading. The meetings occurred in the morning and couldn't last longer than noon because everybody needed to go to lunch. They began to use a formula: a few songs of worship, prayer, announcements, take up offerings, another few songs, and, just like that, they said "goodbye" to the Holy Spirit. The meetings began to center more about man and man's teachings and about man's desires and dreams for ministries, and the Holy Spirit was no longer there.

Up until now, which is 40 years later, every time I go to Bolivia, I find churches that are so structured, cold, and boring, the Holy Spirit is no longer welcome. So many leaders now yearn for the presence of the Holy Spirit, to be a witness of His power and His presence. But, they are not willing to give up their dreams, their ministries, their selfishness, or their lives.

The only vessel that the Holy Spirit will ever use is a surrendered vessel. An empty vessel. In order to get to that position, we need to surrender totally to the Holy Spirit. We need to give up our dreams, our desires, our ministries, our lives, our plans—everything has to be placed at the foot of the Cross.

That is the price that we must pay. It will cost everything.

In John 15:13, Jesus said:

> Greater love has no one than this, that one lays down his life for his friends. You are my friends if you do what I command. I no longer call you servants because a servant does not know his master's business. Instead, I have called you friends for everything I have learned from my Father I have made known to you. You have not chosen me, but I have chosen you to go and bear fruit-fruit that will last. Then the Father will give you whatever you ask in my name.

THE WORD THAT CHANGED A NATION

He did His part by laying down His life for us as a friend. Let us do our part by laying down our lives for Him (Ruibal 153).

We need to understand that this is a divine work, and the Holy Spirit is the only One that is capable and prepared with knowledge and experience. He is the One that will bring unity to the church and prepare a Bride without blemish when Jesus Christ comes back. The Holy Spirit doesn't need our help. We need the help of the Holy Spirit. This will never happen if we structure everything according to our selfish ambitions.

This is a warning for you, pastor; for you, leader; for you, that has a ministry:

Let Him use you—your hands, your mouth, and your life—and stop trying to use the Holy Spirit.

If there is anything that is good in our lives, that's because of the grace of God. It's because Jesus paid the price for us on the cross. It is a gift from God to every believer. We cannot be pure or perfect in our own strength and knowledge. We can only be pure when the Holy Spirit purifies. We can only be good when the Holy Spirit changes our hearts, our morals, and our minds. We can only be holy when the Holy Spirit is the One that has total control of our lives. We need to go back to the Cross.

There, we will know and understand that we are not better and not worse than anybody else. Don't think that you are better than a drug addict, than a murderer, or an adulterer. You are not. You are the same. Only the grace of God is making the difference in your life.

You are not worse than anybody either. We are made out of flesh, with desires and thoughts. We are humans, but if we believe in Jesus, He is the One that is going to transform us with His grace. So all the glory and honor and praise is going to go to Him. We are not going to be able to boast in our strength, our ability, or our knowledge. If we are going to boast, we are going to boast in the strength, mercy, and grace of our Lord Jesus Christ, our only Savior (Galatians 6:14).

CHAPTER 11

THE DESERT:
THE COST OF DISOBEDIENCE

The spiritual explosion of the revival had begun to calm down, and the multitudes began to dwindle. Julio was away preaching in South America at this time. One day, around April of 1973, we were having a meeting in De Monticulo with around 5,000 people in attendance. This was our last large meeting. While we were meeting, it began to rain. Everybody looked for shelter, but there were only two shelters. Of course, everybody fled to whichever shelter was closest to them.

We ended up in two separate groups. While we were waiting for the rain to stop, the Holy Spirit told me, "As these two groups were divided by the rain, there is also going to be a division in the Church."

It was a strange message. I didn't understand it. Others were sent to deliver more warning words to us during this time.

A prophet from the Mato Grosso region of Brazil was sent to our group to deliver a strong message: "Because of your haughtiness and pride, this work of God is going to dissipate." He began to cry as he was talking.

"You need to repent because of your pride. If you do not repent, the power that has been given to you will be taken away, just like the Lord punished His people during the time of the prophets of the Old Testament."

No one paid attention to the prophet or his words.

Amos Anderson, an American missionary we loved and respected, delivered a warning as well. He shined like an angel. I had accompanied him to preach in the jungle.

He prophesied through many tears about what was going to happen. He said, "Oh, oh, you guys don't know what's coming. The sheep are going to be dispersed."

Since we respected him, we did not ignore his warning, but we did not know what to do. We did not know how or when it was going to happen.

While Julio was traveling through South America, he visited Peru, Ecuador, Brazil, Paraguay, and lastly, Colombia. When he got back, it was December 1973. I was the first one that he called. He called me because he had good news to tell me. When I arrived at his father's house where he was staying, he opened the door, and we hugged each other. The feeling was as if I hadn't seen my dad in a long time. I was so happy to see him.

He said, "Look, Fernando, see the newspapers I brought from Colombia. This is what God did in Colombia."

I was amazed and in awe of what the Holy Spirit had done in Colombia. Even the stadiums could not contain all the people. The healings and miracles were the same as in Bolivia. I was so happy to see this.

And then, he said to me, "Fernando, I found what we need in Bolivia. I found the solution to our needs."

"I was in this place," he said, "and I found Paradise. A place where everything is clean. Everything is in order. You won't find a speck of dust anywhere. I have never seen any place like this."

The believers, he said, both the sisters and the brothers, were like angels. Everybody was so immaculate.

"This is what we need here in Bolivia," he declared.

I was so happy to hear this, and I said, "Yes, this is what we need." And then he began to tell me about the place he was talking about.

"After the meetings, this group of believers wanted to talk to me. While I prayed, God told me that I shouldn't talk to them. And that's what I did. But this group was very persistent and waited and waited to talk to me. Finally, I approached them and said, 'I'm not going to talk to you. I have some other things to do.' One of the girls that was with this group began to cry and said, 'Julio, we only wanted to show you what God is doing with us, that's all. Why don't you come?'"

I think Julio was touched by this crying girl, so he decided to go against the voice of the Holy Spirit. He told me, "Fernando, on the way, several weird things happened. We had flat tires, the car wouldn't work, and at one point it was like someone was controlling the steering wheel of the car."

Every time something happened, Julio would rebuke Satan. He thought, "I think Satan is trying to interfere with this because he doesn't want me to see this." So he pressed on and arrived at this place, which he described as a Garden of Eden. That's all he said.

I was happy to hear this from him, and I still don't know why he called me and why I was the first to hear all this.

"How's your family?" he asked me.

"Not too good," I replied.

To me, it was a very hard time because, while I was so involved with God after Julio left for South America, we didn't have anyone to guide us in all the things that were happening. Then my brother committed suicide.

I still don't understand why. God didn't tell me anything. My brother was a Christian and involved with God. This particular day, I remember I was in a house sharing the gospel with some young people. After I finished the meeting, I went home. I saw my dad coming out, and he was crying.

He told me, "Your brother tried to kill himself."

When I got upstairs, I saw my mother crying.

She said, "I'm never going to forgive you. You are responsible for this."

The ambulance came, the doctor came. They tried CPR, but it was too late. He died.

I think one day I will know the reason. My mother grew sick from the shame and the pain, and my whole family was destroyed.

There was such a sense of guilt. We went through all this trauma as a family, and Julio was not there.

When Julio asked, "How's your family?" I replied, "My mother is sick. My brother killed himself. I am to blame for everything."

He said, "Where is your mother?"

"In the hospital."

He went and prayed for her. Obviously, she was sick, physically, and emotionally. Julio prayed more for her emotional needs. They were kissing, crying, and hugging.

That day, I became even closer to Julio. I didn't blame him. I was happy that God was still moving in South America the way that He did in Bolivia. From that day, I was with Julio daily for the next ten days. We had a busy time reconnecting and sharing. Julio was eager to share his discovery with everyone else.

One night, we had a general meeting. It was close to New Year's Eve, and while we were praising and praying, Julio was in the middle of the room. He suddenly collapsed onto the floor. Everybody was scared. He had been away from Bolivia for a long time, and La Paz is a city that is very high, about 15,000 feet above sea level. Everybody thought that he collapsed due to the altitude and the lack of oxygen. So someone took him home.

I went to my house, and the first thing that I did was kneel and start praying for Julio. Because I used to pray for Julio every day, the Holy Spirit would tell me what was going on with him and how to pray.

While I was praying, God spoke to me and said, "Don't pray for Julio because he has sinned. He was not obedient to My command not to talk to this group." I was in shock when I heard this.

He said, "Open your Bible to Jeremiah 17:5." I did so and read:

Thus says the Lord; "Cursed is the man who trusts in man and makes flesh his strength, whose heart turns away from the Lord."

I was unaware that this verse existed because I had just begun reading the Bible.

He said, "Julio is in sin, and every person that has put his trust in him is under My curse."

In this particular passage, when God describes the curse, it is total obliteration, total destruction.

"He is like a shrub in the desert, and shall not see any good come. He shall dwell in the parched places of the wilderness, in an uninhabited salt land."

Jeremiah 17:6

My reaction was, "No! This cannot be."

He said, "I told Julio not to go, and he went. From that, a false doctrine is coming into the church."

I didn't know what to say or what to do. I was in shock.

I stood up, and I said to myself, "I have to tell him."

And so, it was my word against Julio's word. When I said Julio was in sin, everybody got mad at me. When I said that there was a false doctrine, they looked at me like I was crazy. They had all put their hope in Julio.

"Don't talk to Fernando. Don't go near him," Julio told them.

That was one of the hardest times of my life because it felt like I lost my entire family in one day. I had lost my brother, and my family was destroyed. Now I was alone. Nobody would talk to me. They would just look at me and walk to the other side of the street. I felt so lonely, so misunderstood. It was a time of sorrow, of pain. I was so discouraged. I didn't know what to do. All the believers avoided me. I kept thinking, "God, what have I done? I was just obeying You."

Julio said that I was a wolf in sheep's clothing, and so I retreated back and began to wait.

CHAPTER 12

THE POISON OF LEGALISM

The doctrine that came to Bolivia through this Colombian group was one that brought legalism into the Church.

When Julio "found Paradise," he had really joined a legalistic cult run by an authoritative female leader. The group had strict standards of behavior for every area of the Christian life, with the goal of becoming the perfect bride of Christ, without spot or blemish. According to them, only those who lived this way were the true Body of Christ or *Ekklesia*. They began to teach this pursuit of perfection through human strength and doctrine in La Paz. There were rules for everything. The men had to have specific haircuts and couldn't wear shorts. The women wore long dresses and grew their hair very long. Everything and everyone had to be impeccable.

With this goal in mind, everything was analyzed and criticized. Everyone became an enforcer of the rules. Prayers were to have a specific standard. Each person was to be focused and controlled in their actions. Family relationships were destroyed as the group demanded complete loyalty from young people. Believers became suspicious of each other; friendships and unity were destroyed.

Yet the more they tried, the more they found that they were not perfect, and could not be. Condemnation began to settle in the hearts of believers. Many were forced out as they could not become perfect. Some tried to take their own lives. The lives of mature and new believers alike were destroyed. I never saw such destruction in my life. I couldn't believe what my eyes were seeing; I was witnessing the destruction of something very precious to me.

Cursed is the man who trusts in man and makes flesh his strength, whose heart departs from the Lord.

For he shall be like a shrub in the desert, and shall not see when good comes, but shall inhabit the parched places in the wilderness, in a salt land which is not inhabited.

Jeremiah 17:5-6

We could actually write an entire book about this episode. But for reasons of space and time, we are just skimming the surface. Anyhow, I am not the one that is qualified to share this because I saw everything from the outside. From what I could see, Julio's anointing began to fade away. It was like watching a balloon slowly but surely begin to deflate. Julio was not the same. He became authoritarian. He didn't have patience for anything. He used to reprehend anyone and anything. He became mean-spirited. Everybody feared him.

Julio's ministry halted to the point that it became irrelevant. The sad truth is that the Holy Spirit was no longer with him. Nothing supernatural manifested in his life during this time. He was so confused that he began to question everything—even to question the power of the Holy Spirit and to think that what happened in Bolivia was not from God. In fact, due to the influence of the teachings of this group, Julio destroyed almost all of his materials related to the revival. He burned videos, papers, pictures, recorded messages—any evidence of the miraculous encounters that took place. Eventually, Julio established a church, *Ekklesia*, with those who chose to remain with him. The rest of the people left, many forming their own churches, ministries, and fellowships.

So, it was left to me the hard work of receiving all the people that were thrown out from the *Ekklesia* and were totally destroyed. More people began to leave as the effect of the curse of God became more palpable, and the number of those involved in rescue and restoration increased steadily. One by one, we had to share again and again that they were under a curse, needed to repent, and must put their eyes and trust only on God. With that, God began to restore lives. It was a slow process and very painful to watch and live through.

Julio left Bolivia and went walking in the desert for a long time until he finally repented, turned back to God, and returned to Bolivia to ask for forgiveness.

> Shortly thereafter, I left for Bolivia free in spirit, yet still thinking that most of what we had done in Bolivia couldn't have been of the Lord.
>
> It was a very simple trick of the devil. As the Holy Spirit brought understanding to me of His ultimate purpose, I became too critical of myself, taking the blame for not having had the final product.

> *It took some time for God to show me that even though I needed to repent and make things right for the future, I had given what I had. Most of the mistakes I had made were not a problem of integrity, but of judgment.*
>
> *We were inexperienced and first-generation Christians in one of the most demon oppressed countries in the world. Truly, He moved over these nations by His Holy Spirit, anointing an inexperienced vessel in this incredible awakening for the end-time harvest* (Ruibal 61).

After years of ministry in South America, Julio visited Bolivia at the beginning of 1995. He was killed on December 13, 1995, in Cali, Colombia.

I think God, in His mercy, restored Julio's life just before He took him away, perhaps to let him know that He loved him and that he was forgiven. That particular year, he restored Julio with miracles, healings, and honors.

We need to be really careful to see where our hearts are. Our trust should be only in God. If not, we are at risk. I learned that lesson the hard way. The curse did not lose its effect through the years. On one of my trips to Bolivia, I was at a meeting in La Paz, perhaps 30 years later. By then, everything that had happened was a history lesson we all understood.

At this particular meeting, a sister came to me and said, "Fernando, can I talk to you?"

I said, "Sure, let's talk."

She said, "I don't know what's happening to me. I go to church all the time. I give my tithes and my offerings. I pray constantly. I read the Bible. I am a good mother and a good wife. I do everything right, and yet, everything is going wrong in my life. Like everything's falling apart. I don't get it."

Well, I didn't know what to say to that, so I replied, "Let's pray."

I try not to ever give my advice based on the circumstances, knowledge, or experience that I have. I always try to search for the Holy Spirit in these situations.

I began to ask the Holy Spirit, "What's wrong?"

To my surprise, He said, "She is under a curse."

I could not believe my ears. I said, "That was 30 years ago!"

So I said to her, "Do you remember?" I had to remind her of this episode with Julio and the division of the church.

I said, "You are under a curse. You need to repent and ask for forgiveness."

She just looked at me and couldn't believe it. But she was obedient. So she got on her knees, started crying, and began asking for forgiveness. When this sister stood up, she looked totally different. Her countenance had changed. Her eyes changed. It was like I was looking at someone totally different. The change was extraordinary. For the first time in 30 years, she had peace and joy again. I was amazed at the fact that God never changes, and for God, there is no limit on time.

CHAPTER 13

GOD'S HOPE FOR BOLIVIA

During the period of destruction by the legalistic doctrine in Bolivia, God had mercy on me for some reason. I was spared much of the suffering brought on by this false doctrine because I began to travel to different countries in South America shortly after the church began to split. God began to open doors, and the Holy Spirit was with me every step of the way.

I ended up living in Spain for close to three years working with the gypsies. After that, I got married and moved to live in the United States. I didn't go back to Bolivia for ten years. But I stayed informed about what was going on in the church throughout those years.

The first time I went back to Bolivia, I was surprised and sad to see that the church was very divided. Someone from the leadership came to see me, and when I asked, "Do you guys get together often?" they told me, "No. We came together because you are here."

That broke my heart because I couldn't understand how people who had loved each other so deeply didn't fellowship any longer. It was strange for me to see them so divided by their specific doctrines and groups. Before, we had been united through our simple, mutual faith in Jesus and the finished work of the Cross. Division saddens the heart of God.

Now I know, in my personal opinion, that there are two very, very important things to God:

1) For the Gospel to be preached.
2) For the Church to be united.

I am sure that the Holy Spirit is right there working on these two things all the time. I came to understand this through an experience that I will never forget.

One night in 2003, I had a dream.

In this dream, I saw the President of Bolivia at that time, Gonzalo Sánchez de Lozada. He was standing in what appeared to be a pulpit. He began to talk, but nobody was paying attention to him. So he became angry and began to shout. While he was shouting, he was trying to open a drawer, but he couldn't. So, he left. After this, two more men tried to do the same—to talk and to open this drawer, but they were not successful. Nobody would listen to them, and they couldn't open the drawer.

Then, a young man stood up in the pulpit. The appearance he had was very particular of the indigenous people of my country, the Aymara and Quechua. He stood up on the pulpit and began to talk in such a way that everybody paid attention to him. Then he opened the drawer very easily.

My dream ended, and I woke up right away. The presence of God was heavy in my room, and I immediately knew that this dream was from God. The next day, I shared this dream with my wife. She told me that we needed to pray. Now, at this particular time, I was not aware of the political situation in my country. I was not interested and never have been interested in politics. So, everything that I saw was new to me.

In the afternoon, I decided to go to visit my dad. At the time, he was living close to me in an apartment. I used to visit and talk with him almost daily. When I arrived at his house, he turned on the TV to watch the news from South America. The news anchors began to talk about the political situation in Bolivia. I saw that Gonzalo Sánchez de Lozada was having problems, and Bolivian citizens were holding strikes and protests all over the country. The reporter was talking about the tremendous turmoil taking place.

Suddenly, the TV became focused on the young political leader behind the majority of the strikes. When I saw him, I was shocked. It was the same person that I had seen in my dream. I couldn't believe my eyes. The name of this man was Evo Morales. I had a face, and I had a name.

Then, the Holy Spirit told me, "This will be the next president of Bolivia."

When I heard this, I couldn't believe my ears. But I knew that the Holy Spirit was talking to me. So I said to my wife, "This man is going to be the next president of Bolivia."

She said, "Fernando, be careful with the things you are saying. These are very delicate things."

I said, "God is speaking to me."

God told me, "I will raise this man to challenge my Church that is divided."

The tone of His voice revealed anger.

He said, "My Church is going to be united the easy way or the hard way. Men will have to choose."

Well, those were very strong words for me. I could sense that He was really angry, and He meant what He said.

A few months after that, I went to Bolivia for a visit. I shared this dream with some friends and leadership. When they heard this, their first reaction was surprise, then shock. Not at the news, but at my ignorance of the political realm in Bolivia at that time.

They said, "Fernando, you have been living in the United States for so many years. You don't understand what's going on around here. First, you are talking about Evo Morales. He is a leader who is totally uneducated. He didn't even finish elementary school. He is totally ignorant, unprepared. He doesn't even know how to talk. Secondly, he does not have the money, nor the resources to do this. Thirdly, even if he tried, we are sure that the United States will not allow this to happen. So, please be careful, and don't say this to anyone because your reputation is at stake. You are just showing us how ignorant you are."

I was very grateful for their advice. I said to myself, "I am not sharing this with anybody else."

The last night of my trip, we had a big meeting in a church. While I was sharing, the Holy Spirit came to me and said, "Fernando, tell them. Tell them the dream."

I said, "No. I'm not going to ruin my reputation."

He insisted. He was very persistent. When He is persistent, you cannot say no to the Holy Spirit.

So I said, "Okay. Here goes my reputation."

In obedience, I shared everything with the whole church. I will never forget the looks on their faces. There was complete silence. They were looking at me as if I was the craziest person they had ever heard. They began to shake their heads.

I felt very, very bad. I said, "Okay. My reputation is gone."

I got back to the United States, and after three years, Evo Morales, in a supernatural way, became the president of Bolivia. I still couldn't believe it. That got my friends' and the leadership's attention. They wanted to talk to me now.

God told me, "Fernando, go back to Bolivia and share with them that My heart is broken because My Church is completely divided."

Perhaps, many believers don't understand the issue of division because they were born into a divided church. The Church in the United States has been divided for hundreds of years now, and everything is still divided. But the Church in Bolivia from 1977 has only existed for 40 years. All the leadership was raised up at the same time, during the revival. Everybody knew each other when the Church began. As a matter of fact, they shared everything, and they loved one another deeply. However, over time, ambitions, rivalries, and doctrines divided everything and everyone.

So, I was obedient. I went back to Bolivia. When you are obedient to the Holy Spirit, your life becomes an incredible adventure. That was the case during this time.

I called a friend of mine who has connections with leaders from different denominations in La Paz. I told him, "God told me to come to Bolivia and share about the unity of the Church."

He said, "Okay, I'll get in touch with people."

Now, you need to understand that I don't have a big church in the United States. I am not a pastor. We have small meetings at my house. I have been sharing God's heart with different pastors and leaders in Athens, Georgia, where I reside, for several years. Also, I am a paramedic. That is my work. God blessed me with that work.

So, perhaps the few people that knew me in Bolivia were from the revival. But the rest of the leadership did not know who I was. They decided to hold a large weekend retreat at a hotel close to Lake Titicaca.

The night before the conference was to start, the interdenominational pastors and leaders in charge of the conference wanted to talk to me and get to know me.

When I sat with them, the first question that they asked me was, "Are you a pastor?"

I said, "No, I'm a paramedic."

"Have you written any books? Do you have any materials?"

I said, "No."

"Do you have an agenda for the retreat?"

I said, "No."

"What are you going to talk about?"

I said, "Unity."

They were in shock. They began shaking their heads and talking about me amongst themselves as though I was not in the room.

"Who is he? He doesn't have an agenda. It's too late to cancel. He doesn't even have a message prepared."

When I was talking to the leadership, one of the leaders I knew told me, "Fernando, we have tried this so many times, and nothing has ever happened. You are wasting your time."

I said to him, "Nothing has happened because you were trying. But, when the Holy Spirit tries, everything is possible. There is nothing impossible for God."

He didn't like my answer very much, so he left.

To my surprise, the rest of the group said, "Okay, we are going to move forward with the meetings."

I guess they didn't have a choice. When it comes to His agenda, the Holy Spirit can persuade anyone.

All the pastors from different denominations had decided to take buses to the meeting together to save fuel and money. All the buses arrived at the hotel, which was far away from the city. You could not walk to the location, and there were no other means of transportation to that place. After the buses arrived, the bus drivers said they were having some problems, so they were going to have to drive the buses back to the city. That meant everyone was stuck at that hotel.

The meeting began with dinner, and the attendees sat in groups of their own denominations. Nobody spoke to one another. The atmosphere was incredibly tense because many guests had hurt or been hurt by one another. It was almost impossible for them to pray, not even to bless the food because they not only disliked one another—they hated each other.

I was really worried. I was thinking, "I don't know what I am going to do." I prayed that night with my wife, asking God to help us because anything less than a miracle would achieve nothing.

The next morning after breakfast, we got together, and I was introduced to the group. I grabbed the microphone, and everybody was seated in a way where they could see one another. When I began to speak, one of the Aymara pastors stood up, and he said to me:

"You are not a pastor. I am the one that should be talking, not you."

And then, the pastor that was by his side stood up as well, and they both began screaming and shouting.

I do not recall any more details, but they were very angry with me. Everybody was looking with their mouths open, and the place was very tense.

I began to pray and ask the Holy Spirit, "Help me, please. What can I do or say?"

The Holy Spirit told me, "Wash his feet."

I said, "What?"

He said, "Wash his feet."

I said to this pastor, "Can I wash your feet?"

He screamed at me and said, "You will never, ever touch me!" He became angrier.

So the Holy Spirit said, "Ask him again."

I said, "Can I please wash your feet?"

I think he said, "Are you deaf? Do you not understand what I am saying? I said, 'No! You will never ever touch me!'"

They began to talk about how they had been mistreated.

I was very confused. I didn't know what to do. I was fearful. I asked the Holy Spirit, "Please, what can I do?"

"Ask him again."

For the third time, I asked, "Can I please wash your feet?"

He looked at me and said, "If you're going to wash my feet, I'm going to wash your feet."

Breakthrough! I was so relieved. I said, "Sure. Can someone bring me some water?"

I took the water. I took off his shoes and put his feet in the water. He began to cry. I began to cry. Everybody was crying. I was asking him for forgiveness.

I looked around, and, inexplicably, the pastors began to wash one another's feet and ask for forgiveness. The Holy Spirit began to move in such a way that He began healing hearts. That was the beginning of three glorious days during which I saw how powerful and merciful God is and that He really, really wants to help His Church to be united.

After the washing of the feet, everything changed. They really forgave, forgot, and recognized that they were brothers and sisters. They began to laugh, make jokes, and harmony was evident in everything we did. People who had hated each other began to hug each other. It was easy to share the food and give thanks. For our last meal, we shared communion bread and wine. The presence of God was so tangible, and everyone had peace and joy in their hearts.

Now I understand why the voice of God had been filled with anger when He spoke to me. The division ran deep among His people—hatred was a part of their everyday life on every level. It was not just division about doctrinal matters, but also division along racial lines. Just days before this meeting at Lake Titicaca, I remember talking with some Aymara pastors who would meet in a very humble place. The floor was dirt, and all they could share was a cold drink and a piece of bread.

They all looked at me as if they were thinking, "What's this white guy doing in here?"

After I shared with them about the dream I had and about unity, I remember one of the pastors told me, "When I invite the white pastors to my church, I try to honor them and give them the best I can. I let them sit in places of honor, and I treat them with much respect. But when I go to their congregations, because I cannot speak proper Spanish and because my wife dresses differently, they offer us the worst places to sit. They feel ashamed of us in their meetings" (James 2:1-6).

At this, he began to cry. He was a grown man, and he was crying like a little child. That particular night, my heart broke. How can the church be divided in such a way? I totally understood why God was so angry. We should treat our brothers and sisters with much love and respect because the price over each of them is the death of our Lord Jesus. That's how precious they are before our Father. We are brothers and sisters. We believe in Jesus, and the love of God is in our hearts.

I know that there is nothing impossible for God, and ever since that time, I have been traveling through the years to different parts of Central and South America as a witness that God is healing and uniting His people. The Holy Spirit is very much involved in that. He has to be. Our Lord Jesus Christ is coming very soon, and He is coming for One Bride, One Church.

Every believer in this time needs to understand how important the unity of the Church is to God. We need to be aware of and work on it. We need to pray for it and seek unity everywhere we go because, in the times that are coming, we are not going to be able to survive if we are divided. We need each other now, more than ever. We need to be able to understand and see how God looks at the Church. He sees us as one body, made of many members. It's about time for us to understand there is one Body, one Faith, one Church (Ephesians 4:4-5). We need to put more emphasis on that and not on personal ministries or ambitions (Ephesians 5:4-6).

I think we are obsessed with growth and numbers, but not with quality. We are obsessed with megachurches, but it is so sad because those gatherings are more like social events than anything else. People don't know each other. People don't love each other. And we call this a "big ministry."

To me, it's just men feeding their egos with their love of power and popularity. We crave those things. We like to think that without us, the Church cannot work properly. Let me tell you something: no one is indispensable. God needs all of us, not just a few of us. We don't have a monopoly on God's power, love, or plans. Sometimes we even think we have the monopoly on the Holy Spirit.

It is time for us to repent and throw away our egos, our plans, our ministries, and hear and understand with a humble heart what Jesus was praying about before His death.

John 17:20-26 says it all:

I do not ask for these only, but also for those who will believe in me through their word, that they may all be one, just as you, Father, are in me, and I in you, that they also may be in us, so that the world may believe that you have sent me. The glory that you have given me I have given to them, that they may be one even as we are one, I in them and you in me, that they may become perfectly one, so that the world may know that you sent me and loved them even as you loved me.

Father, I desire that they also, whom you have given me, may be with me where I am, to see my glory that you have given me because you loved me before the foundation of the world.

O righteous Father, even though the world does not know you, I know you, and these know that you have sent me. I made known to them your name, and I will continue to make it known, that the love with which you have loved me may be in them, and I in them.

That's what's in the heart of God: the unity of the Church. If that's not our goal, we are missing the point. We are missing the goal that God has in His heart.

The Church of Jesus Christ is one Church that does not have a name and does not belong to a man. The Church of Jesus Christ belongs to

THE WORD THAT CHANGED A NATION

God Himself. Jesus Christ paid the price with His life, to be able to have one Church, one Body, one Bride. The Holy Spirit is always working to fulfill the prayers of our Lord Jesus Christ—for the Church to be one like He is one with the Father. The sinful and selfish desires of our heart can often get in the way of this unity, which is why He warned us to beware of false teachers and teachings (Matthew 7:15, 2 Corinthians 11:13).

PHOTO GALLERY

Julio César Ruibal
1953-1996

Ruibal's Presence Achieved the Consecration of Everything in Town

La presencia de Ruibal logró la consagración de todo un pueblo

Ayer domingo se repitieron los prodigios

Rubial's meetings were marked by the repentance and return to faith of thousands.

*Julio César Ruibal Prays for Entire City:
50 Thousand People Witness Miracles*

*Inspired by Jesus' Command to Love,
Ruibal Cries Out for A Renewal of the Faith*

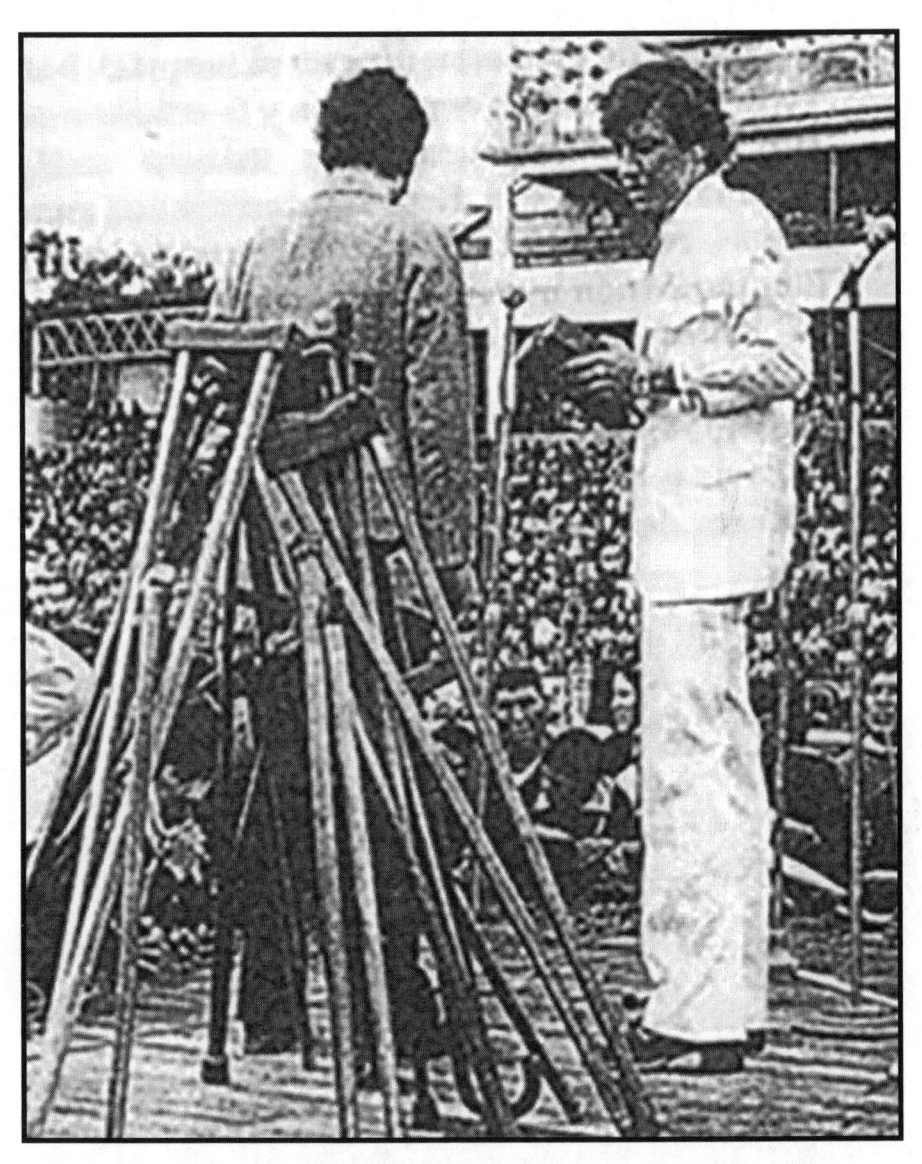

Julio César Ruibal standing next to multitudes of abandoned crutches
January 14, 1973

The healings were taking place in such proportions that thousands of crutches, canes, orthopedic prosthetics were left behind after the meetings. The healings were for everyone, including the military, natives, farmers, etc.

— Julio César Ruibal

I Was Listening to the Radio While Ruibal Was Praying, and I Was Healed

Interview with Angel Quijarro Viscarra
January 11, 1973

Ruibal Impresses Well, Although There Were Skeptics

Stadium meeting in La Paz
January 14, 1973

"Faith Healed Me," Said Many Invalids After Ruibal Prayed

"LA FE ME CURO" DECIAN MUCHOS LISIADOS LUEGO QUE JULIO RUIBAL ORO

Julio praying for the sick
January 20, 1973

Julio surrounded by the sick
January 14, 1973

Imposing View of the Multitudes at Ruibal's Third Meeting

Imponente marco humano en el tercer oficio de Ruibal

Ruibal's third meeting in La Paz
January 21, 1973

*Thousands of People Spent the Night Outdoors:
25 Thousand Entered the Stadium*

Julio's Mother Remained Outside the "Siles Stadium"

Last meeting in La Paz stadium
January 1973

Julio preaching
January 14, 1973

PART II:
LESSONS LEARNED

CHAPTER 14

PERSONAL LESSONS

Because of the magnitude of the revival in Bolivia, the needs were gigantic. Everybody was searching for God and looking for leaders and churches. As I said before, we were not prepared for any of this. There were hundreds of thousands of people who had so many questions and were looking for a place to fellowship. Through all of this, we learned many lessons. Some were very painful to learn. Some were very useful. Some were very fulfilling.

The Holy Spirit began to teach us individually in so many ways. He's the best Teacher ever. There is no one like Him. He is an expert in everything, especially in the Word of God, since He is the author of the Word (John 1:1-2).

When I began to read the Bible, there were portions that I understood and others that I didn't. I didn't have any teacher to go to. Julio was not in Bolivia anymore. The leaders were as ignorant as I was about the Word of God. The Holy Spirit became a Teacher to me with this one verse that I didn't understand. I began to pray constantly about this verse.

Blessed are the poor in spirit, for theirs is the Kingdom of Heaven.
    Matthew 5:3

The more I read this verse, the less I understood it. I knew that the Holy Spirit was my Teacher, so I began to pray and talk to Him. I don't remember how long I waited for Him to answer my prayer, maybe a couple of months.

One day, I was playing my guitar in my house and worshipping God, and then the Holy Spirit asked me, "Fernando, do you still want to know the meaning of this verse?" One thing I have learned about the Holy Spirit is that He always talks to me when I least expect Him.

I said, "Of course, what does this verse mean?"

The Holy Spirit said, "It's very simple, Fernando. How would you describe someone poor?"

My reply was, "Someone who is poor does not have anything. He doesn't have a house, a car, a bed to sleep in, or clothes to wear. Not even anything to eat."

I knew what a poor person was like because, at that time, my country was one of the poorest countries in South America, so I was exposed to poverty.

The Holy Spirit said, "Yes. Now how would you describe someone who is rich?"

I said, "Someone that's rich has many houses, many cars, the best places to sleep, the best food to eat, lots of money, the best clothes. He doesn't just have shoes, but Italian shoes—handmade."

The Holy Spirit said, "Yes."

He asked me another question, "How would a poor man react if you gave him the leftovers from your table?"

I said, "Well, he would just grab the food and say thank you many times and perhaps hug me or kiss me or kiss my hands. Then he would eat and enjoy the food and have gratitude in his heart."

"How would a rich man react if you did the same and gave him your leftovers?"

"He will feel very offended. Perhaps he would throw the food in your face or on the floor and let you know that he has the best food. That would be his reaction and his attitude."

And He continued to ask, "What would a poor person do if you put a mattress on the floor and told him he could have that used mattress on the floor?"

I said, "He will feel so grateful to be able to sleep on something soft and warm. On the other hand, the rich man would feel offended and angry and let you know that he has the best bed, not just one, but several."

He asked, "What would a poor man do if you gave him your used shoes? Even with a hole in one of the soles?"

I replied, "The poor man would be happy and grateful to have something to wear so the cold floor would be away from his feet. The rich man would perhaps throw that pair of shoes in your face and let you know that he has the best shoes ever."

I began to understand clearly that He was talking about the attitude of our hearts.

He said, "Someone who is poor in spirit is someone who is grateful for everything and anything that comes to him. He is always grateful to God."

I was in awe of the simplicity, wisdom, and depth of this parable. I began to see how ungrateful my heart was and how I needed to change my attitude. I began to worship Him and say, "Thank you. Thank you, Holy Spirit, because now I know what 'poor in spirit' means."

Then He said, "Fernando, this word is for your brothers in Argentina. You will go and share this with them."

That, I was not expecting because I had never traveled outside my country before, much less flown on a plane. Three or four years later, I was on my way to Europe, and I had to stop in Buenos Aires, Argentina. I decided to stay there for several days. By then, we had contacts with one of the largest churches in Buenos Aires, the church where Juan Carlos Ortiz, Angel Negro, and Jorge Imitian ministered. I had come with Angel, who was the pastor of this church of 3,000 people. I was very curious to see this church and how the service was conducted. I was sitting in the very back, just observing people.

Suddenly, Angel said, "There is a brother from Bolivia that is here. He will come here to the front and share something with us."

That caught me by surprise. I went all the way to the pulpit, and I forgot the lesson that the Holy Spirit had wanted me to share about being poor in spirit when in Argentina. As I grabbed the microphone, I was praying and asking, "What do you want me to tell them?" like I always do.

The Holy Spirit said, "Remember what I told you about being poor in spirit? Share that with them."

I shared in simple terms what the Holy Spirit had taught me years before. To my surprise, everybody began to cry, and then they came to the altar to repent. I didn't understand what was going on. I could see that this particular word was powerful for them, that it was bringing them to their knees.

After everybody composed themselves, Angel said, "I have heard this verse explained in so many meetings through preachers with doctorates in theology, but I have never heard something like this."

They were in awe at how simple and profound this verse truly was. One thing that we truly need to understand and actually repent for is the fact that we ignore the Holy Spirit so much in everything. He is by our side 24 hours a day. He is the author of the Scriptures. And yet, we ignore the author, and we jump onto our computers and search the Greek, the Hebrew, the different people with Ph.D. degrees that supposedly know the Word. We trust in them and not in the Holy Spirit. He is the best Teacher.

We need to be totally conscious all the time of His presence in our lives. Something that we learned during the revival was that the Holy Spirit was there in a tangible way—always exalting and praising the name of Jesus Christ. We got used to the feeling of His presence.

As a matter of fact, that was the only thing that we were searching for all the time. If we prayed together, we were looking for His response right away. If we praised, it was for Him to be manifested in a tangible way. We needed to feel the presence of the Holy Spirit. We used to talk amongst ourselves in these terms, "Did you feel the Holy Spirit in the meeting? Was His presence there?" It was a matter of physically and emotionally perceiving His presence.

Because of the revival, so many preachers and teachers wanted to come and see what was going on in Bolivia. Pastors from Argentina came, and one of their first teachings was about feelings. They said, "You guys are always talking about feelings. We shouldn't live by feelings because we need to live by faith."

It is written, "The just shall live by faith."

Hebrews 10:38

Of course, they knew much more about the Bible than we did. They used so many verses, and they taught us in this way. Suddenly, we stopped searching for the tangible presence of the Holy Spirit because everybody believed we needed to live by faith, without feeling anything. This had a negative effect on so many people because they literally forgot about the presence of the Holy Spirit.

Another lesson that the Holy Spirit taught me is that He is a Person. Jesus Christ called Him "He." He didn't say "it." And we use "he" only when we are referring to a person. So the Holy Spirit is a Person who is real, who has feelings, thoughts, and plans, who can be grieved and pleased. When we talk to or spend time with a person, we feel their presence.

When my wife is at home, I can feel her presence even if I don't see her. I know that she is near. When she comes and sits beside me, I can feel her presence, her warmth. I can hear her voice. I can have a conversation with her. It would be crazy for me to say, "My wife is by my side by faith." That's not natural. Either my wife is by my side, or she is not. It is the same with the Holy Spirit.

As a human being, I have a soul, I have a spirit, and I have a body. Emotions and feelings are part of the soul, and we have a lot of soul in us—lots of emotions, lots of feelings, and we use language more than anything else to communicate feelings and thoughts. We are always expressing something that we are feeling. We shouldn't suppress our feelings because, remember, faith will always produce something.

Now faith is the substance of things hoped for, the evidence of things not seen.
Hebrews 11:1 KJV

Faith is not just a word. Faith is a substance that we take into the presence of a God who is alive, and into the presence of the Holy Spirit who is here with us all the time. And so you will feel Him. You have to feel His presence. For us who came from the Catholic Church, we once perceived the Holy Spirit as a ghost—a mist in the air. In my personal view, the Holy Spirit was an invisible presence. When I began to understand that the Holy Spirit is a Person, my perception and experience of Him changed completely.

Jesus identified the Holy Spirit as a Person. He clearly speaks of "He," and said it would be better for Him to go because He would send "Another," meaning "Someone like Himself." Someone of the same nature. The presence of a Person with whom you can talk, walk, and feel. You begin to have a relationship with a Person who is alive, a Friend, a Teacher, a Guide, and Counselor (John 14).

You know what? When He manifests Himself, everything changes. The atmosphere changes, and we know that we are before Someone who is holy, pure, and awesome. I think that this is just one lesson that we all need to learn. This Person has a voice.

He who enters by the door is the shepherd of the sheep. To him, the gatekeeper opens. The sheep hear his voice, and he calls his own sheep by name and leads them out. When he has brought out all his own, he goes before them, and the sheep follow him, for they know his voice. A stranger they will not follow, but they will flee from him, for they do not know the voice of strangers.
John 10:2-4

When I first gave my life to Jesus during the revival, I didn't know that He spoke. Nobody told me that. Then I began to hear His voice, and I began to recognize and trust His voice. I didn't know yet what Jesus said about this in the Bible, that we would recognize His voice so we can follow Him (John 10:27). The Holy Spirit is our Guide. It is impossible to follow a guide if you are not listening to his instructions. To me, it is very important for you to learn to recognize His voice.

When I was traveling to different countries and visiting different churches, people began to ask me how to recognize the voice of the Holy Spirit. I tried to explain the best that I could, but perhaps my explanation didn't make much sense to them.

One day, the Holy Spirit gave me this example:

"What happens when a woman gets pregnant? The first thing that the woman does is hold her belly and talk to the baby. This happens for nine months, normally. After that, the baby is born. When the mother first holds the baby, she begins to talk to the baby. And she talks and talks for two years, perhaps. Usually, the baby begins to speak his or her first words around a year or a year and a half. For a year and a half leading up to speaking, plus nine months in the womb, the baby has been hearing the voice of the mother.

"If you place a blindfold over the eyes of a three-year-old child and gather 100 women, this boy or girl will easily recognize the voice of their mother. Why? Because he or she has been hearing the mother for a long, long time."

It is the same with the Holy Spirit. How much do we listen? How much do we hear Him? As a matter of fact, we don't even spend ten minutes a day trying to hear Him. For us, prayer is to go somewhere, perhaps to the church or house, and we talk and talk and talk and talk for 30 or 40 minutes. And then we leave.

We call this "prayer time."

A prayer is a conversation between you and God. Usually, a good conversation goes both ways. You have to talk, and you have to listen. I think the less you talk, and the more you listen is even better. God, in His wisdom, gave us two ears and one mouth. We need to listen twice as much as we speak. Even nature can tell us this much.

In the beginning, it will be strange that you are listening to a voice. In the supernatural world, there are so many voices. There are voices of angels. There are voices of demons.

It will be confusing in the beginning. The more you listen, the more you will be able to recognize the voice of the Holy Spirit (John 10:4-5).

One thing is for certain, the Holy Spirit will never tell you something that is not in the Word of God. He will always take you to the Word when He talks to you. So in that way, we can rest safely because we have the Word of God at our disposal to make sure that we are hearing the voice of the Holy Spirit. Little by little, you will be able to recognize His voice more and more.

We are living in dangerous times that are going to get worse. We are going to have to rely on the direction of the Holy Spirit. For me, it is of the utmost importance that you are able to listen and discern the voice of the Holy Spirit. That is something that we learned during the revival. We saw the power and the love of God. We understood that He is very much alive and that He speaks to people. So we began to rely on His voice and to trust and to obey Him.

One day in 1974, the Holy Spirit told me that I needed to go to Cochabamba.

I said, "Okay."

I knew that He was going to provide for my needs, including the ticket to go to Cochabamba. I was in a meeting, and from this meeting, I walked all the way to the bus station. It was strange because people came to me and handed me money. They were total strangers to me.

"Here, have this money, have this money," they told me.

By the time I reached the bus, I had enough money for my one-way ticket. I knew God was with me, and He increased my faith. God provides in a supernatural way all the time. We shouldn't ask for offerings. We shouldn't ask for support. Instead, we should trust in God with all our hearts.

At the station, I asked the Holy Spirit, "Which bus should I take? Which seat should I sit in?"

He told me the name of the bus and the seat number I should sit in. I purchased my ticket, got on the bus, and soon arrived in Cochabamba. I had never been to Cochabamba, and I had no contact there. I had to rely on the Holy Spirit.

Once I arrived, the Holy Spirit told me to walk straight. So I did, until I heard, "Stop."

Then I heard a different voice say, "Go to the right."

I went to my right and felt something really funny. I knew it was not the voice of the Holy Spirit. So I stopped, and I heard this laugh. I knew the enemy was trying to deceive me.

So I asked again, "Where should I go?"

The Holy Spirit said, "Go to the left and keep on walking until I tell you to stop."

And I walked for I don't know how long. And then He told me to stop. He said, "Fernando, do you see that door in front of you?" It was an apartment with several floors.

He said, "Go to the second floor."

On the second floor, there were four doors. He said, "Go to the second door from the left and knock." The door opened, and in front of me stood a friend of mine from the revival.

He just looked at me and asked, "What are you doing, and how did you get here?"

I told him, "The Holy Spirit sent me here to help you."

That is how the Holy Spirit began to lead us whenever we would travel. During and after the revival, I went to Chile, to Argentina, to Spain. Even now, I continue to listen and obey Him whenever I travel. His voice is so familiar now. Everything He tells me is true, and I feel so sure and secure because He is reliable and the best Guide ever. He is the best GPS with all the updated information. To walk with the Holy Spirit is an adventure—the greatest adventure. You see His hand, His protection, care, and love.

At that particular time, the revival was still going on strong in Cochabamba. God had sent my friend César to preach the gospel in this particular city. When I arrived, I found that the Holy Spirit was touching so many lives. Many people, particularly high school students, began to know Jesus Christ. Healings and miracles were happening every day, and there was a strong move of the Holy Spirit happening in Cochabamba, a city that would become a refuge, an oasis for believers during the hard times that were soon coming over the church in Bolivia.

The believers were really young but full of the zeal, love, and presence of God. Truly, it was an honor and privilege to go to Cochabamba to help César. That is the Holy Spirit as a Guide.

When you begin to have a relationship with Him, it's like a relationship with someone you love very much. If you're not married, it could be your mother, father, your sister, or brother. Or if you are married, your husband or wife. It is a close relationship. You begin to understand when He is happy or when He is sad. It is the same as in your house. If your wife is sad or happy, you will understand this quickly. You don't need her to speak, you can sense it. Nobody has to tell you.

It is the same thing with the Holy Spirit. You can sense when He is grieved and when He is happy. He is very happy when you are humble, dependent, and obedient to His voice and His direction. We need to open our hearts, search for the presence of the Holy Spirit, and have a relationship with Him that is so close that, in the end, we just become reflections of His grace, love, and power.

Julio was not even a year old in the Lord when the revival began. However, in that year, the Holy Spirit allowed him to grow in a supernatural way. He knew much more than his years as a Christian reflected. He was given supernatural wisdom, the gifts of the Holy Spirit—not only healing, but words of prophecy, wisdom, knowledge, and every other gift were actively demonstrated in his life. He also knew the Word—He was always quoting scripture.

The Holy Spirit spoke through Julio's mouth every time he spoke. When he was guided by the Holy Spirit, his leadership was flawless, and everybody could perceive the power, wisdom, grace, and anointing that was with him because it didn't reflect his 19 years. Julio spoke to presidents, the press, gave interviews, and spoke at conferences. The wisdom that he displayed was supernatural.

Once during a time of prayer, the Lord gave me a vision to explain His anointing on Julio's life.

Jesus was by my side, and I saw Julio walking and talking as a 19-year-old in his white suit.

Jesus told me, "I want you to talk like Julio. I want you to walk like Julio."

I said, "I'm not Julio!"

He said, "That is not Julio, but my anointing on Julio."

The message that I received was, "Let My Holy Spirit cover you completely so that you will walk and talk like Me."

From that time, 45 years ago, I have never seen that anointing on anybody else. I have met anointed people, but never to the degree that Julio was.

When we talk about anointing, we have many ideas about what it is because we don't understand what it really is. When the Old Testament speaks of anointing, prophets and kings were covered, or smeared, with oil on the outside of their bodies. In the New Testament, when the Holy Spirit first came, He filled the Upper Room, then the people inside—His presence covered the people completely.

When the anointing comes, you are only a reflection of the Holy Spirit, Christ, and nothing else—you reflect His grace, His personality, His power. It is not you but the Holy Spirit over you to the point where you are not merely yourself anymore. People around you can perceive the anointing—"something is different about you; something is special about you."

When we talk about anointing, we are talking about personality—the mind, how we talk, how we walk, how we interact with people. Your mannerisms change to become a reflection of Christ, His power, grace, and wisdom. The whole character of Christ comes upon you.

The Church doesn't understand this anointing. The more time you spend with the Holy Spirit with a genuine heart, the more His anointing will be over you. The Holy Spirit is always in you, but the Holy Spirit will also be over you. That is what Jesus was talking about (John 14:17). To me, the anointing comes when the Holy Spirit is on the outside. The more you trust in the Holy Spirit, the more fruit you're going to have (John 15:5).

The more you are exposed to cigarettes, the more you are going to smell like cigarettes. The more time you spend with the Holy Spirit, the more you are going to carry the fragrance of Christ (2 Corinthians 2:15). Julio used to pray and stay with Him from eight in the morning until eight in the evening. He was secluded with the Holy Spirit before the revival. He was always praying all day long.

To me, the anointing comes with different levels for different people. I see these different levels of anointing when Elisha, the prophet told Elijah, "I want double your anointing" (2 Kings 2:9). The life that a regular Christian has been called to live is a life with the anointing of the Holy Spirit. It may not be at the same level that Julio or Elisha had, but there is going to be some level of anointing, to the point where people are going to notice and ask, "What is it you have? There's something different about you. I want to have that too."

The anointing is perceived even more by the world because that is something totally strange for them. We are all called to live in some type of anointing because the Holy Spirit is with us. We can seek this anointing, and I think that is why Jesus used to pray for hours and hours with His Father. The anointing that Jesus had was being renewed and being poured on Him more and more—that's my perception.

The amount of time spend with Jesus = His anointing over you

It is not that you are trying to achieve the anointing; anointing comes by grace. But when you begin to spend lots of time with the King of kings, sooner or later, His fragrance will cover you completely (2 Corinthians 2:15).

As a matter of fact, we make a mistake to seek the anointing of God with impure desires and dreams about the things we will do with it. It is like we are looking for and seeking the hands of Jesus instead of searching for His heart because we equate anointing with doing. We need to equate anointing with being and not doing. When you love Jesus and surrender to Him for who He is, His anointing will flow naturally. We do not search for anointing through Jesus; we search for Jesus, who is the Anointed One.

CHAPTER 15

FROM UNITY TO DIVISION

How can we understand what happened in Bolivia during this time? How could such destruction take place?

In the beginning, unity was naturally birthed from the revival. Everything was to glorify the name of Jesus because He only has one Church, one Bride. We relied upon the guidance of the Holy Spirit in everything. We were led by the Spirit and loved by the Spirit—He brought freedom, love, and joy to our lives. That was the fruit of unity.

After that, the division came—the division came through legalism that brought condemnation and took away the freedom, the joy, and the love. The destruction of unity came about from very good intentions. Julio's intention and dream was achieving perfection: our lives ought to be perfect, our prayer lives, and our praise had to be flawless in order to please God.

The intentions and the goals were biblically-based and sounded "good," but the method to achieve this perfection was not because it was based on human strength, human reasoning, and human methods and goals. I think that the enemy uses legalism by taking advantage of the good intentions of leaders and ministries. The result was total division and destruction of the believers. We had the opportunity to both enjoy freedom and endure legalism in Bolivia and to see the results of both.

We knew that the only way to achieve perfection is through the grace of God and the strength and anointing of the Holy Spirit because where the Holy Spirit is, there is *freedom*, joy, peace, and justice (Romans 14:17).

> *It is for **freedom** that Christ has set us free!*
> Galatians 5:1 NIV

> *Now the Lord is the Spirit, and where the Spirit of the Lord is, there is **freedom**.*
> 2 Corinthians 3:17

The destruction in Bolivia was sudden, very dramatic, and brutal because Julio didn't consider maturity, gender, needs, or weakness. He didn't consider any of these because there was no mercy. The message was: "Either you are perfect, or you are out."

The end result was the discovery that nobody could be perfect, and the aftermath was destruction, suffering, and division. And so, the words of Jesus Christ became more clear when He said, "I'm the vine, you are the branches. Apart from Me, you can do nothing" (John 15:5).

We forgot that we needed a Savior every day. He is the only One who can save us from ourselves—from our weakness, from our sins. He is the only One who has the ability to make us perfect. It is through His grace, mercy, and love.

The division came very quickly and suddenly—in about six months after Julio returned, everything was divided and destroyed. People were kicked out based on their prayer lives, Bible reading habits, and form of worship. If you didn't meet the standard, you were unworthy and unfit to be a member of the *Ekklesia*. Julio even left and fled to Colombia for a few months because he could not meet his own standard. By the time he came back, all the old leadership had left. Only eight people remained; some members were as young as 16 years.

Many people left to preach the gospel in separate directions, raising up different groups. They pursued ministries, money, power, and their own interests. Thousands of groups arose in Bolivia, but they were all divided from one another. Members of each group had no interest in communing with other groups.

I left Bolivia for Spain during this time. After three years, everything had changed entirely. There was Julio's *Ekklesia* and a thousand other groups. After that, I came to the United States and didn't return for ten years, but while I was away, even more groups began to emerge. By then, they had all criticized each other over members, money, TV and radio stations, popularity, fame, or whatever. There was not only division, but even hatred began to form in the hearts of the believers. It was like two parents had gotten a divorce, and the children were all separated and failing to continue in relationship with one another.

Despite this, God is raising up a new generation who only care about seeking the glory of Jesus. For them, division is a foreign word that they don't understand. They have no problems gathering with anybody. The problems come from the leadership. Even now, the leadership only come together when I come into town once every year or two. They understand the purpose of unity intellectually, but they cannot attain it by their own strength or ability.

We can be together without being united. When we are together, trying to be united out of our own strength, I think the main things that hinder unity are the love of money, power, and personal ministries. We need to have the following mindset:

It's not my church, but the church of God.
It is not my ministry, but God's ministry.
It is not my money, but God's money.

When we understand that what we have has been given to us by God, we can share everything.

CHAPTER 16

THE CHURCH IS ONE

We thought this was normal—no denominations. In the beginning, we were one family, one Body in Christ, with no divisions. The trademark of this church was true fellowship, the love that existed amongst us. God gave us the grace to be one family. My wife, Laura, was born again two years after the start of the revival, and she was able to witness this unity.

> *One time I was going to Cochabamba and the people in La Paz met in the bus station with guitars, worship, and prayer to see me off. The spiritual family would surround every person coming or leaving with prayers and blessings. This genuine sense of family came only through the grace of God. For sure, we didn't know what we had. We thought the church loved like this and had this sense of unity everywhere.*
>
> *We were in prayer all the time for each other as well. The Lord had a supernatural connection where He would give dreams and visions revealing how we needed to pray for our brothers and sisters, no matter how far or near they were.*
>
> —Laura Villalobos

We learned that unity does not only develop physically, but also spiritually, when each member of the Body has his or her heart set on seeking Jesus above all else. False unity arises when Christians seek community over Christ. Believers can seek unity through the same skin color, nationality, social background, doctrine, or interests. When we seek this type of unity, a false community is formed—not a family.

The seal of the Holy Spirit on this revival was pure unity. We were able to witness and enjoy that unity. The Bible describes the Church as a body. The human body is completely connected, and the Church is also completely connected spiritually. We can experience each other's emotions and bear one another's burdens.

*For we **were** all baptized by one Spirit into one body ...*
                                                    1 Corinthians 12:13 CSB

You see, this verse is written in the past tense. The Holy Spirit is always going to bring unity to the church because that is His main role and His main ministry. The Church is not paying too much attention to this. When we talk about the Holy Spirit, we talk about gifts, miracles, and power but we forget what is most important to the Holy Spirit—unity.

Ephesians 4:1-3 HCSB states:

*Therefore I, a prisoner of the Lord, implore you to walk in a manner worthy of the calling you have received with all humility and gentleness, with patience, accepting one another in love, diligently **keeping** the unity of the Spirit through the bond of peace.*

Keeping, not *creating* unity, because the Holy Spirit has already made us one. Our calling is to **keep** the unity of the Spirit with the peace that binds us. Actually, we didn't know this then. It was a grace supernaturally given to us in the revival—we perceived unity as normal.

Now, looking at the church so divided, it is clear we are not listening to the Holy Spirit or following His guidance—our role is to maintain unity because Jesus looks at His Church as one. He is coming for one Church only. It is critical for us to understand this.

We were already baptized into unity; it is our job to maintain that unity. There is nothing man can do to create unity. The only One who can create unity is the Holy Spirit. He confirms this message with signs and His presence, bringing healing whenever I have preached it in so many countries. Impossible things begin to happen as part of this unity. One of the first signs of revival, more than anything else, is unity, because it is one of the main ministries of the Holy Spirit. Consequently, one of the main goals of the enemy is to bring division at any cost. That is why the Church is so divided now.

Great destruction came upon the Church in Bolivia, and the church was divided and scattered. The prophecies that God gave us came to pass. We need to be aware that we are in a state of spiritual warfare 24/7 and that the enemy is not playing. He is trying, by all means, to destroy the Church, to bring division to the Church, and he will use doctrine, money, power, sex, and religion.

What we witnessed in Bolivia was the power of God being manifested in such a way that we were astonished by how powerful He is. Also, by His mercy, grace, and favor. In reality, we understood that truly, really Jesus Christ is the same today, yesterday, and forever (Hebrews 13:8). He is the One that will never change (James 1:17).

We were also witnesses to how much destruction the enemy can bring to the Church. In this case, destruction came through doctrine that was very difficult to discern and through the door of a seemingly small act of disobedience to God's voice on Julio's part. The price that we had to pay was very, very high, with lots of casualties—division, sorrow, loss, pain, and condemnation.

Jesus clearly said:

A house that is divided against itself cannot prevail
Mark 3:35

That's what is happening in the Church.

Bolivia has witnessed the extreme love of God and also the extreme hate of Satan. Forty or more years have gone by already, and some of the leadership that persevered through many trials and tribulations are now pastors of large and medium-sized congregations, or smaller groups. The work of God continues—mostly through human effort and knowledge. I think we can count on one hand the groups and churches that totally rely on the Holy Spirit.

CHAPTER 17

GRACE UPON GRACE—WALKING IN THE SPIRIT

In traveling through Latin America for so many years now and getting to know different ministries and pastors in leadership, there is one desire that drives the hearts and minds of the believers—how to obtain the anointing of the Holy Spirit, the tangible presence and power of God.

That begins a never-ending search to have an encounter with God. I have been asked so many times, "What can we do to obtain the anointing of God?" "Is there a method to it?"

The people that are asking these questions are precious sons and daughters of God who are committed to Him in love and service. We have a deep-rooted desire and tendency within us as human beings to "do something" in order to obtain what we are looking for. This was ingrained in us by our parents as children.

"If you want to achieve anything, you have to do something. If you go to school, you have to study hard in order to obtain good grades. You obtain good grades in order to go to a good college. You go to a good college to obtain a good profession. You obtain a good profession to make the most money that you can in order to live comfortably." These are familiar words spoken all over the world.

So everybody thinks in this way. It makes sense and is very logical. When we come to God, we come with the same mentality. That's part of our nature—working hard to become something. In order to understand where this tendency originates, we need to go back to the beginning, when God created Adam and Eve. They were happy and had a perfect relationship with God. They had a perfect environment. God walked and talked with them. But when they disobeyed God and sinned, something happened to their minds.

The first thing they noticed was that they were naked. Knowing that God was going to come to talk to them, their first reaction was to cover their nakedness with leaves. That was the first time that man did something in order to be with God. Before their sin, they didn't have to worry about this. They didn't notice that they were naked, and they had a wonderful relationship with God. He provided everything, and they needed nothing. They didn't have to do anything to earn that relationship. They just had to enjoy His presence.

But after they sinned, they began to do things to earn His approval and affection. First, they covered themselves. Eventually, men began to make up altars to sacrifice things to God in order to please Him. Ever since, man has been trying to do something to obtain the presence, blessing, and favor of God. To me, that desire to earn things from God is the root of legalism, which is embedded so deeply in our nature. That's why it is so hard to recognize its presence in our relationship with God. We can only clearly see its negative effects when it is taken to the extreme, usually after it is too late.

Think about why we have so many religious cults, false doctrines, prophets, and leaders. Whether it's sacrificing, fasting, or keeping the law, we are always trying to do something for God's love and approval.

But when Jesus came, He came to show us what grace meant because, according to John 1:15-17, John bore witness about Him and cried out:

> *This was He of whom I said, 'He who comes after me ranks before me, because He was before me." For from His fullness, we have all received grace upon grace. For the law was given through Moses; grace and truth came through Jesus Christ.*

Jesus was full of grace, and we are receiving from His grace constantly. This means that we don't have to do anything to earn anything. The things of God are free. Jesus Christ paid the price for everything on the cross. There is nothing else that we can add to His sacrifice because He paid for everything. Now the only things that we need to do are believe and receive.

To believe or to do? These two are mutually exclusive. Either you believe, which leads you to do good from a place of freedom and gratitude, or you do in order to earn favor, good gifts, or God's love.

When it comes to the Holy Spirit, I think that the disciples were exposed to many miracles through the hands of Jesus. I am very sure that they felt the presence of the Holy Spirit. That's why Jesus at some point told them:

> *"And I will ask the Father, and He will give you another Advocate to be with you forever—the Spirit of Truth. The world cannot receive Him because it neither sees Him nor knows Him. But you do know Him, for He abides with you, and He will be in you.*
>
> John 14:16-17

Before Jesus was crucified, He told His disciples that His Father would not leave them as orphans and would send Someone to console them and guide them (John 14:18). I don't think the disciples knew what to expect. All they knew was that the Holy Spirit was going to come, and they were supposed to wait in Jerusalem (Luke 24:49).

They were gathered waiting and praying in fellowship. Suddenly, without warning, the Holy Spirit came and surprised them. They didn't do anything to deserve or earn the promise of the Holy Spirit.

Well, after that, they thought that they had the ownership of the Holy Spirit and that the Holy Spirit was only going to be given to the Jews. God, in His mercy and wisdom, surprised them again. When Peter was sent to Cornelius' house, while he was talking, without any warning or any expectation or plan, the Holy Spirit came and touched the Gentiles. Peter was in shock (Acts 10:44-46).

The rest of the disciples couldn't believe it.

From then on throughout history, we know that the Holy Spirit always surprises us. All the revivals were in places that the Holy Spirit chose through people that the Holy Spirit chose. Yes, some of the people were praying and searching, but they did not have a clue when, how, or where the Holy Spirit was going to come. That was the case in the Welsh Revival, Azusa Street, East Timor, Indonesia, and Bolivia.

In our case in Bolivia, we were surprised by this move of God. It went against our logic and nature. We only saw the truth through the Bible, and the experiences believers had when the Holy Spirit surprised them. We were not looking for revival. We were normal people living normal lives in the world without God. We were blind to the reality of the love, power, and mercy of our Lord Jesus Christ.

I'm sure that many people were praying for the revival, but they were not expecting the magnitude of the revival. They were not expecting the place of the revival—much less expecting that God would use a 19-year-old as His instrument. All of this was a surprise for us.

From then, and through the years, I began to have something clear in my mind: the things of God are from grace, to grace, and for His glory. He is the One that chooses places, people, and time. We need to understand that our Father is a sovereign God. He does things according to His will, and we cannot force His hand—no matter what we want or try to do.

When God moves, He uses earthen vessels full of flaws, and it's only His grace that is able to compensate for these. If we could understand this, then it would be easy for us just to relax and abide in Jesus Christ and be ourselves—not pretending to be anyone else or trying to force the hand of God or trying to produce the move of the Holy Spirit by our own strength and knowledge. This is impossible.

There are so many different testimonies about healings and wonders in Bolivia. When I share these, I can perceive the minds and hearts of those listening, trying to understand and frame it so that they can manipulate and recreate it through human strategy. God did not come to Bolivia because we were prepared or because we had knowledge, but because of His mercy and grace for this dying world.

Recently, I heard a testimony that I didn't even know happened to a friend of mine. He was very young then; the event happened more than 40 years ago.

One day he came home, and he was met by his live-in maintenance man who told him, "Your bird just died."

He said, "Just throw him in the trash."

The maintenance man said, "Well, you talk and preach about God, and you pray for sick people. Why don't you pray for your bird?"

He was surprised by this statement. Then he thought, "Well, I don't have anything to lose; I'm just going to pray for the bird."

He prayed for the bird, and the bird came back to life.

He was in shock and surprised. He was not expecting this to happen. It was something God did to show him that He was alive. He didn't fast for it. He didn't perform any special spiritual rituals to prepare for it. Certainly, he was not expecting that to happen. God was using regular people—not mystics. He was using their hands. He was using their mouths. But it was God Himself who was behind it.

We cannot do or say anything without God backing His Word up. He is the only One who can heal, revive, save, and resurrect. We need to understand this and just relax and abide in God (John 15).

We must pray, seeking His face and not His hands, seeking His heart and not searching for fame. We need to humble ourselves before Him and surrender everything to Him. Only then will God have an instrument in His hands He can use according to His purpose. I think this is the greatest need in the leadership and the entire Church today. This is just the beginning of breaking free and healing from legalism.

There is NOTHING that we can do to find God in our own strength, knowledge, or gifts.

There is NOTHING we can do to force Him to use us as an instrument.

He is the One who chooses His instruments. The only thing that's left for us to do is to live by His grace and not by works—to enjoy His love and mercy every day. Only then can God fill our hearts with His presence and love.

Living by grace doesn't mean living in sin. It means that only Jesus by His grace can change our sinful human nature. Only He can transform us and make us pure and holy—without self-effort (Romans 6:1-2). To me, that is the biggest miracle I have ever witnessed; to see how God can transform a life—totally and completely. Living by grace means to abide in Him and to be with Him because apart from Him, we cannot do anything (John 15:5). That's what He told us:

The atmosphere of the Kingdom of God is joy, peace, and justice in the Holy Spirit.

Romans 14:17

Every time that we humble ourselves and search for His heart, these things will come to us. The Holy Spirit is going to remind us that Jesus Christ paid for everything on the cross and made us righteous before God. That is the justice of God. It is not our justice.

I think that the Holy Spirit wants to remind us of this all the time. We need to go back to the cross to truly understand what justice, redemption, and salvation mean. Those are big words we use but seldom understand. Yet these are practical words to live by every day. That is the abundant life Jesus was referring to—to live in total freedom from ourselves, our circumstances and the world—only in Jesus can we be free (John 10:10; John 8:36).

CHAPTER 18

SONSHIP OVER SERVITUDE

One month before the Lord led me to Cochabamba, while I was praying, the Holy Spirit began to reveal to me what it means to be a son of God. I had been a Christian for many months, but in my opinion, God was far away. I didn't know until that time that I was His son.

This concept had never crossed my mind, and nobody ever talked to me about it. It was something new, a shock to me. One of the things the Holy Spirit does when He comes into your life is to lead you and teach you that you are a son of God.

For all who are led by the Spirit of God are sons of God.
Romans 8:14

And because you are sons, God has sent the Spirit of his Son into your hearts, crying, "Abba! Father!"
Galatians 4:6

Well, that particular night, the Holy Spirit was not just giving me mere information about these verses. He revealed to my heart and mind what they truly mean. That completely changed my life. From then on, I understood that I have a Father who loves me unconditionally because I am His son, and I can't do anything to earn or lose that love.

In the beginning, the revelation came through my mind. I began to think about the fact that I was a son. Obviously, I understood what it meant to have a father because I had a good natural father who always took care of us. So my concept of a father was very high because I had the blessing of having a very good father.

After I understood that concept, then it was like the Holy Spirit was introducing me to my heavenly Father. At the beginning of my life as a Christian, I had a clear relationship with Jesus and the Holy Spirit—but God the Father was far away. I did not yet know my Father in Heaven as a son. That came by revelation. At that moment, I could feel His love for me as a Father. Then I could see that His love was completely unconditional. I felt that love, and I understood that love. Now that I am a father, I understand that concept. I love my daughters because they are my daughters, not because of what they do or what they think, but because of who they are. My love for them is unconditional.

But then came the revelation that I had the nature of God within myself because I was His son. I was born again from Him. Something happened in my mind, almost like brain surgery. It is one thing to understand this. It is another thing to have this conviction come alive deep within. It is like you have never met your Father before, and someone grabs you and takes you and tells you, "That's your Father." And the Father is looking at you, and you can feel His presence, you can feel His love. You can see that He is looking at you. And when He embraces you, then you realize that you really, truly belong to Him.

What then blows your mind is the understanding that all the resources of heaven belong to you. All the inheritance that Jesus received has now become yours (Luke 15:31). He not only embraces you, but He takes you and shows you, "This is your house, these fields are yours, and all these servants." He shows you everything in your inheritance. And then you experience all that within you.

It's like someone is inflating a balloon inside of you, and your head actually lifts up because you are proud to have that Father now, and you see the power that is behind you. You can walk with such confidence, and you know that your Father is listening to your prayers. You know that He is so powerful. He owns everything in the world. He holds the universe in His hands. He has given everything to you.

When the Word says God is our "Abba," it implies a very intimate relationship, bringing us into the highest standing before our Father. I didn't lack confidence before this, as I was proud to be my father's son. But that was nothing compared to becoming a son of my Father in Heaven. I was a son of the King. It was not pride. It was not arrogance. It was just the assurance that God is my Father.

I also understood that He gave me the freedom to walk, talk, and behave like a son of God. I knew that I had privileges and also responsibilities. But truly, I didn't have to do anything to earn this position. I don't have to do anything to earn it or reach it or have it. It was given as a gift to me. That took a burden off my shoulders—that I have to do something in order for God to use me. God uses me because I'm His son, and I have access to all the resources of heaven at His disposal

(Luke 15:31). I entered a new dimension. To me, my perception of God changed. I don't know how long I was there praying and crying because God was doing so many things in my mind and my heart.

I remember the next day, my mother saw me and asked, "What happened to you?"

I asked, "Why?"

She said, "You look different. You talk differently. You behave differently."

Only then did I realize that God had done something inside of me so that I became a new person. I noticed that my mind was different; my convictions were stronger. The way I spoke was different. The way I walked was different. My friends could also see the change.

"What happened to you? You have changed," they said.

The presence of God was so tangible. We can teach about sonship, but only the Holy Spirit can truly change your whole mind and heart, especially if you have a difficult background or experience with your father.

I remember my first trip after understanding this concept. I was in a meeting in Cochabamba, and there were many believers attending the meeting. As always, we grabbed hands, and we began to pray. My prayer that afternoon was very simple: "Father, thank you for your presence. Thank you because we are together." That's all I said.

We began to cry and to shake because the presence of the Holy Spirit was so tangible. We stayed in that presence for a long time, just praying and enjoying Him, nothing else.

After the meeting, one young man came back to me and said, "Fernando, that was so easy. You didn't even have to pray, and God moved. The other people have to pray for 30, 40, 50 minutes, and God still doesn't move."

That was kind of shocking to me at first, but then I understood—we don't have to impress God with our prayers or our spirituality. He knows our hearts and our minds. He moves because He is pleased to move.

Jesus was so clear about this in John 14:18; "I will not leave you as orphans; I will come to you."

The ONLY commandments we have to keep are to love our Father with all of our minds, with all of our hearts, with all of our strength, and to love our neighbors as ourselves (Matthew 22:37-39), because God is love (1 John 4:8).

From then on, I did not try to impress anyone with my prayers. I knew the Holy Spirit would move because I was God's son. I still don't think that God will move because my prayers are so eloquent. On the contrary, I know that God will move because He promised that He will manifest Himself to us. We cannot control God or make His presence tangible, even if we try.

Three years ago, I attended a men's conference in the United States, hosted by Lee Grady, former editor of Charisma Magazine, for pastors and leaders from around the world.

I only went to this particular conference because my son-in-law called me and asked, "Do you want to go to this conference?"

To which I said, "I really don't want to go to any conference. I just want to stay at home with my wife and daughter."

Then he said, "Please come with me because it's in Georgia, only an hour and a half from your house, and I do not want to go alone. I want to be with you."

I went to pray and asked, "God, can I go?"

He said, "Yes, you can go."

I don't just go to meetings or events because people invite me but because I'm looking for the will of God.

When I got there, my son-in-law, Ives, introduced me to Lee Grady, and we sat for dinner at a table with people from different parts of the world. They asked me, "Tell us about the revival in Bolivia."

I was surprised. How did they know about the revival in Bolivia, which was over 40 years ago? Lately, for some reason, the revival in Bolivia is coming to light, and many people are talking about it. As I began to talk a little about the revival, suddenly God gave me a word of knowledge for a pastor from Germany. I began to speak to him, and he began to cry.

Everybody was kind of surprised at what was happening. I was not part of the conference. I was just an attendee.

Lee asked me, "Can you do me a favor?"

I said, "What?"

He said, "Can you pray for us at the end of the last session before everything finishes?"

I said, "Sure, I'd be honored to."

When the time came, I don't remember calling people to the altar. I was just talking about the revival in Bolivia, sharing testimonies of the things that Jesus did in my country.

I said, "The same Jesus is here with us today."

Suddenly, the entire atmosphere changed. People began to cry and rush to the altar in repentance. Everybody was crying aloud, wailing. They came rushing to the altar—crying, praying, repenting. They were experiencing what we experienced in Bolivia 40 years ago—the tangible presence of the Holy Spirit convicting their hearts. Obviously, that was a total surprise for me.

I didn't have anything planned, as I didn't know that I was going to speak. I did not make an altar call. I did not ask for music to be played to create a certain atmosphere. Certainly, I was not trying to manipulate anyone's feelings. I was just sharing who Jesus was. God disrupted that meeting, and I wasn't even able to stay. I left the meeting, and everyone was undone and feeling the presence of the Holy Spirit.

I knew one thing—that if God wanted to use me, I needed to be surrendered to Him. We cannot take credit for this. God loves His people so much, and God loves the world so much that He wants to touch and change lives forever. Now, those are things that He does of His own will. There is no way that we can manipulate the Holy Spirit to do such a thing. That's His plan, that's His will. The only thing we need to do is be obedient and to share whatever is in our hearts. The rest is in God's hands.

Only the Holy Spirit can bring His people to true repentance. Only the Holy Spirit can touch hearts and open minds. There is no such thing as a heart of stone for the Holy Spirit. When He touches someone, that person can feel the power and the love of God.

For a long time, God told me not to pray in public. I found that usually when I am with people, I would pray in a completely different way than I do when I am alone with Him. He showed me that most of my public prayers involved talking to the people in the room to please or impress them instead of truly crying out to Him with a humble heart and pure intentions.

> *When you pray, you must not be like the hypocrites. For they love to stand and pray in the synagogues and at the street corners, that they may be seen by others. Truly, I say to you, they have received*

their reward. But when you pray, go into your room and shut the door and pray to your Father who is in secret. And your Father who sees in secret will reward you.

Matthew 6:4-6

Only when He had stripped me of my pride by prompting me to pray in secret could He then trust me to pray in front of others. Later, I would pray only if someone asked me to. The Lord would always move in great power in response to a simple, heartfelt prayer. By teaching me to pray in secret, He could then reward me in the open because I finally understood that He is the only One who is powerful. If He moves in power, it is because of His great love for His people and not due to my own effort or eloquence.

CHAPTER 19

THE PRESSURE IS OFF

We cannot convince anyone that the Gospel is true. The Holy Spirit is the only One who can convict the world of sin, righteousness, and judgment (John 16:8). We need to understand that the Holy Spirit is the only one who can touch hearts, convict of sin, open the eyes of the blind, and reveal the Gospel to people. That's His job, and He is an expert at doing that. We make the mistake of trying to help Him. We try to convince people about God. We try to convict people of their sins. Obviously, this is not going to work.

I was introduced to this lesson by the Holy Spirit during the revival. One day after I had given my life to Jesus, as I was walking in the streets of La Paz, I ran into a friend. I approached him and gave him a hug. Orlando was very bright and smart. I knew that he was going to be very successful.

I said, "Orlando, how are you doing? It's been a long time since I saw you."

He said, "Fernando, I'm doing very well. I'm studying to be an engineer. I'm in my second year of college, and I'm already an assistant to my professor."

I was glad to hear that. I said, "Orlando, I knew you were going to do something like that because you are so smart."

Then he said to me, "What are you doing?"

I said, "I'm preaching the Gospel."

He looked at me and said, "Have you lost your mind? Don't you know that God doesn't exist? You're wasting your life and your time."

He became very agitated and angry. "Many of you Christians came to try to convince me of God's existence. But you know what? I convinced so many that God doesn't exist. I know so. I am the president of the Communist Party at San Andrés University. God does not exist. God is a creation of the human mind, and Americans invented Jesus. If you are going to try to convince me, you are going to waste your time."

I said to him, "Orlando if I were to try to convince you, it is going to take me so much time to do it. On top of that, I would have to be very, very nice to you. That's not my role. I know Someone Who's going to convince you. It's the Holy Spirit. Orlando, Jesus loves you, and Jesus is alive."

He looked at me and said, "You are crazy."

He turned around, did not shake my hand, and disappeared.

After a week, my phone rang. It was Orlando on the other end.

The first thing he said was, "What have you done to me?"

He said, "Fernando, I cannot eat. I cannot sleep. I cannot do anything. There is a voice telling me that God loves me, and Jesus is alive. All day for a week. I don't know what to do."

"Orlando, it's easy. Just open your heart to Jesus. Give your life to Jesus."

He gave his life to Jesus while we were talking on the phone. The next week he was baptized in water. To me, that was a big lesson. It's not my role to do the work of the Holy Spirit. That is His privilege alone. Mine is just to preach the Gospel. The Gospel is good news. What is the good news?

At Pentecost, Peter, full of the Holy Spirit, spoke about who Jesus was. He ended up saying, "God has made that same Jesus, whom you crucified, both Lord and Christ." At this, all the hearts were touched by the Holy Spirit, and they said, "What can we do?" (Acts 2:36-37). That's how the Church was born.

To me, preaching the Gospel is announcing that Jesus is alive, that He was resurrected, that He loves us, and that He is Lord of lords, King of kings, and He is coming back very soon. That's the only thing we are required to preach. The rest is in the hands of the Holy Spirit: to convict of sin, judgment, and righteousness (John 16:8-13). Only He can bring people to true repentance. He is an expert at doing that. Preaching the Gospel should be very simple and straightforward. It is simply announcing who Jesus is. People need to put their eyes on Jesus, not on themselves, and rely on the work of the Holy Spirit.

When we began to preach the Word in Bolivia, we didn't know anything about how to preach the Gospel. The only thing we could say was "Jesus loves you. Jesus is alive. Jesus is coming back very soon."

That was it. I never knew where that came from, but everybody said that.

When the guy prayed for me, he said, "Who wants to know Jesus?" He said, "Touch him," and God touched me and saved me.

THE WORD THAT CHANGED A NATION

The last time I went to Cochabamba, we were talking about how Jesus touched our hearts during the revival.

One brother said, "Well, everything started in houses. We were in the world; we didn't know anything about Jesus.

"Everyone was either on drugs or into philosophy. This guy who was a drug user went to see Julio because everyone was talking about Julio. He looked at Julio and said, 'Look, I have something much better than Jesus. You're going to love it.'

"He took his pipe, he put marijuana in it. At that time, everyone was using recreational drugs.

"He said, 'Here. Do you want to smoke?'

"Julio said, 'Look, I don't need that because I have Jesus. And Jesus loves you.'

"The people that were around the guy saw him fall to the floor. When he stood up, he was a Christian."

Another time, an atheist was going to argue with Julio from his Communist Manifesto. "Look, I have my Little Red Book," he said.

Julio said, "Look, Jesus loves you."

He simply touched him, and he fell to the floor.

We saw that in Julio, so that's the way we all preached the gospel. With power. He seldom condemned people.

"We are dying," Julio would tell people. "Where are you going to go after this life? Jesus is your savior. Jesus will heal your body, but your soul is more valuable. Do you want to go to heaven? He is the only way."

For the kingdom of God does not consist in talk but in power.
1 Corinthians 4:20

CHAPTER 20

THE REALITY OF THE CHURCH

Idolatry of Ministry

Everything was given to us by God. We do not possess anything, God possesses everything. As ministers and leaders, we need to understand that we are also part of the Body of Christ and not just friends of the Body of Christ. If we think we are servants or friends of Jesus but lack the understanding of being members of the Body of Christ, we will be left behind when Jesus comes. We are part of the Church; a gift, a ministry was given to us only to serve the Church (Ephesians 4:11-16).

Everything that was given to us was given to minister to the Body—our primary calling. The purpose of the parable of the talents is to make more talents for God and His people to do what He wants. He can take our talents away and give them to other people if we are unfaithful (Matthew 25:14-30).

The gifts He gives us are for His church everywhere—not for ourselves or our own selfish ambitions (1 Corinthians 12:7).

That was the first test Moses had to pass as he led God's people. In Exodus 32:7-12, Moses had to stop and pray, "God, they are not MY people, but they are YOUR people." Moses could have said, "You're right; they are my people." That's the first test we need to pass: I don't own anything. If I have something, it was given to me by God, but it belongs to God. All of our gifts and talents are His.

Jesus doesn't get paid for being the Shepherd of the sheep. That's why He gave His life for the sheep—the one who is getting paid for taking care of them doesn't care for the sheep. They leave when the money disappears, and the sheep get eaten by the wolves (John 10:11-13).

Sadly, the Church is about numbers now: how many people I have in my church = how much money I am going to have in my purse. That is a hindrance to unity that the enemy uses all the time. It is getting even worse. Jesus is coming soon, and now is the time in which Jesus is separating the wheat from the tares.

Prosperity Gospel

Over ten years ago, I was watching a Christian program on TBN, when I heard a preacher. I was impressed by the way that he was preaching with so much passion, conviction, and eloquence. I began to enjoy what I was hearing. Of course, everything was based on the Word of God, and he was explaining that whatever you sow for the Kingdom of God, you will reap. For example, if you "sow" thousands of dollars, God will multiply that and give it back to you. In essence, every believer can become rich through this method.

He ended his sermon by saying, "You cannot outgive God."

Bring the whole tithe into the storehouse, that there may be food in my house. Test me in this," says the LORD Almighty, "and see if I will not throw open the floodgates of heaven and pour out so much blessing that there will not be room enough to store it.

Malachi 3:10 NIV

Give, and it will be given to you. Good measure pressed down, shaken together, running over, will be put into your lap. For with the measure you use it will be measured back to you.

Luke 6:28

I began to get very, very excited because it was based on some truths found in God's word, so I truly began to enjoy the sermon.

I said, "This has to work. I'm gonna try this."

Suddenly, the Holy Spirit talked to me with His simple words. "Fernando, where do you want to store your treasures? Here on earth or in heaven?"

He reminded me about the words of Jesus when He spoke about seeking riches in heaven instead of earth and how we cannot serve two lords; we cannot serve both God and money (Matthew 6:14, 20).

The conviction of the Holy Spirit broke me. I began to search my heart and truly meditate and think on these words. After much seeking, I understood, clearly, how the enemy was going to try to use this prosperity teaching to deceive the Church. From then on, I began to hear testimonies and reports of how the Church was reacting to this message. Everybody wanted to put this teaching into practice because it actually works. The essence of the teaching is rooted in the Word, and it's based on God's promises. I began to see my fellow brothers and sisters sow money, cars, houses, properties—everything.

God is always faithful to His promises. The people that sowed in money received back much more than they gave. The people that were sowing cars received back many more—the same thing with houses and properties. Greed began to set into the hearts of the Church. Everyone became obsessed with material things, and people began to compare each other and judge the spirituality of their brothers and sisters based on the material goods they received from God.

They were beginning to say, "Well, this brother gave $1,000, and God gave him back ten times more. He must be close to God. He must love God so much. This brother gave his house, and God gave many houses in return." And so on until corruption began to set into the Church, and this doctrine received its infamous name—the Prosperity Gospel. By then, I saw clearly where God stood with it, and what the Word said about it.

> *Do not lay up for yourselves treasures on earth, where moth and rust destroy and where thieves break in and steal, but lay up for yourselves treasures in heaven, where neither moth nor rust destroys and where thieves do not break in and steal. For where your treasure is, there your heart will be also.*
>
> Matthew 6:19-21

Where is it better to have your riches? In heaven or on earth?

If you are going to heaven—or hell, for that matter—you're not going to be able to take anything from here. So what are you going to do with ten houses or ten cars? Or millions of dollars? Where are you going to take it? Nowhere. It's so sad. Much of the church leadership all over the world got involved with this, not just in the United States. It didn't stop there. It went much, much farther than that.

They began to say, "If someone is sick, or you are sick, if you sow something, the sick person is going to be healed."

People began to seek healing through material things. They forgot that Jesus died on the cross so we can be healed. He died on the cross so we could have eternal life. We cannot buy His blessings with material goods. That is blasphemy in the face of God. We are rejecting the most precious sacrifice that God gave to us—His only Son.

Jesus Christ is our example, and He will always be our example. On earth, He did not own anything, did not have a bed to lay His head to rest. He was amongst the poor. And yet, in heaven, nobody will be richer than He. If you are seeking material things, you will find them. But I don't know if you would be able to get to heaven, and if you do, you're going to be very poor in heaven. Jesus was very clear about that. And I think He knew what He was talking about.

Satan is going to use lies to separate us from God, and a lie—a very good lie—contains at least 10% truth. It is sometimes difficult to discern, but when Satan comes with the Word of God, we are going to be deceived if we don't take care. Deception comes when Satan uses the truth of God to make us fail. When Jesus was tempted by the devil, the devil used the Word of God to try and deceive Him (Matthew 4:1-11). In this particular case, teachers and preachers are using this Word to deceive the church.

Be careful where your heart is. You cannot serve riches and God.

No one can serve two masters: for either he will hate the one and love the other, or else he will be loyal to the one and despise the other. You cannot serve God and money.

Matthew 6:24

Now he who received seed among the thorns is he who hears the word, and the cares of this world and the deceitfulness of riches choke the word, and he becomes unfruitful.

Matthew 13:22

Then Jesus, looking at him, loved him, and said to him, "One thing you lack: Go your way, sell whatever you have and give to the poor, and you will have treasure in heaven; and come, take up your cross and follow Me." He was sad at this word, and went away sorrowful, for he had great possessions. Then Jesus looked around and said to His disciples, "How hard it is for those who have riches to enter the Kingdom of God!" And the disciples were astonished at His words. But Jesus answered again and said to them, "Children, how hard it is for those who trust in riches to enter the Kingdom of God! It is easier for a camel to go through the eye of a needle than for a rich man to enter the kingdom of God!"

Mark 10:21-25

It is sad to see that the Church now, in general, is looking for earthly, material things. That's the only thing we talk, and think about. It's time for the Church to repent and start searching for the things that are eternal, that are divine. We need to start asking for the gifts of healing, prophecy, revelation, and we need to start building treasures in heaven. Our life on this earth is very short. Sooner or later, one day, we will be facing Jesus, and we will be judged for everything that we did and everything that we said. Nothing is going to be hidden from Him (Revelation 20:12-13).

Brothers and sisters, we are not from this world. We belong to the kingdom of God. Seek to store up treasures in your heavenly home.

Commercializing the Things of God

This is a subject that could be a pitfall to ministries and churches. While writing on this subject, we must look at it from different points of view to try to convey what is in God's heart in a balanced manner.

While traveling through Latin America and the United States, I have noticed that people with good intentions at the beginning ended up, because of greed, using God's things, the things that are holy, for their own benefit. This should be just a warning of what not to do and where to go.

The root of the problem is greed, which is part of human nature. When we come into the Kingdom of God, subtly, that greed accompanies us. How can we understand the extremes to which ministries and churches have already gone? We have plenty of examples around the world. I have only questions that we need to ask ourselves because those questions, I think, are going to be asked by Jesus on the Judgment Day.

How can we justify having mansions instead of houses? How are we using the money that God has provided through regular, obedient, and humble people who, each month and each week, give to the church? Are we good administrators of the wealth that God is providing to the church?

I think this is a very thorny and touchy subject. We understand that we need the financial resources to expand the Kingdom of God. The problem is, as always, our hearts, our intentions, our motives.

We understand that "the laborer deserves his wages" (1 Timothy 5:8). That's what the Bible says. If you are a laborer with the laborers of God, what is your salary? How much money do you need to make a living? To provide for all your needs? We know that God is going to provide our needs. The problem is when we are looking for more than our needs.

If you are making a living by being a pastor, look at your heart. Beware of the greed that is always there. If you are making a living as a composer, as a singer or musician, again, look at your heart. Are you simply providing for your needs, or are you going way beyond that? Remember, we are using God's money, not ours. There is a need to examine these practices in light of scripture.

Due to the prosperity gospel doctrine, we are now justifying excesses, and it is now all about money and material things. Money, in itself, is not evil. But the love of money—it's evil (1 Timothy 6:10).

Are you working because of the money or because of Jesus? Are you singing because of the money or because of Jesus? Are you writing books because of Jesus or because of the money? Search your heart. Even better, ask the Holy Spirit to search your heart.

Brothers and sisters, be careful of this because God is going to demand every penny from each of you (Matthew 5:26). Remember, Judgment Day is for everybody and, sooner or later, we are going to face Jesus.

I give this message with much love. If there is something you need to repent of, repent because there is so much at stake—your well-being here on earth and also your inheritance in heaven.

I may have said this before, but we learned this lesson through Julio. He could have been a very, very rich man, but he chose to give everything away for the glory of God. I can say that greed was not Julio's problem. He spent all his resources to magnify the name of Jesus. It is hard to find people with that heart in these times. I pray that God will open your heart, give you wisdom, and bring you to a place of balance.

As always, for some reason, we think that Jesus changes all the time and that in this particular thing, He has also changed. Let me tell you something—He has not changed, and He will never change. He gave this commandment to His apostles to preach the gospel:

Heal the sick, cleanse the lepers, raise the dead, cast out demons.
Freely you have received, freely give.

Matthew 10:8

Everything that has come to our lives through the gospel has been, is, and always will be FREE.

When God began to move in Bolivia during the revival, we understood this clearly: that Jesus paid the biggest price ever at the cross—His own life—for us to receive the gospel and the baptism of His Holy Spirit to perform healings, miracles, wonders, and receive eternal life.

Everything is free of charge because the price was already paid.

The revival in Bolivia was never about money, rewards, or favors. It was always about grace.

The revival in Bolivia didn't cost a penny, and it was free because it was given by Jesus Christ. Julio could have, but never sought riches or fortune. He understood that everything had to be given by grace and for grace—in other words, free of charge.

When God took Julio to heaven, he didn't have much to leave to his family. As a matter of fact, he left very few things. He received everything by grace and gave everything by grace. What we see now is the opposite.

Many pastors, preachers, and ministers are trying to use the things that God gave them free of charge to make personal fortunes. They charge a fee for anything and everything. From the simple things to the most complicated things, everything is about making money. They are seeking to start megachurches because of the money they are going to be able to generate.

They write books because of the money they are hoping to bring in. They write songs, trying to make money. So, the church has become like a marketplace in which we offer the things of God as merchandise. We sometimes even offer rebates or sales. We advertise God's things saying, "If you register for this conference ten days earlier, we are going to give you a 30% discount. If you bring more than 20 people at this conference, we are also going to give you a discount."

With music, we offer concerts, and we charge at the gate—$50, $70 and even more.

People who have the gift of music and writing worship songs that are inspired by the Holy Spirit are selling these gifts that were given to them for free in order to make money. We are merchandising the things of God that are holy and sacred. A song that was inspired by the Holy Spirit with words and music belongs to the Holy Spirit and should be shared freely because it was given freely.

If you are a composer of these songs, did you have to pay the price to get that composition into your heart? You didn't pay a cent. But don't you ever forget that Jesus paid the price for this on the cross so you can share this inspiration with the church, your brothers and sisters, and not use something that was given to you for free to make money and to become rich.

It is the same thing with books. Why do we write so many books? Is it not to make money? "If I write this book and sell 1,000 copies, I'll make this much money. I hope it becomes a best-seller, so I can become rich."

We fail to understand that spiritual books are inspired by God in your heart. Those gifts are given to you free of charge. What you write should be given free of charge. Everything is given by God through grace, and we receive by grace. We should give it to others by grace as well.

We organize Christian conferences with the goal to make money. Two years ago, I was in Mexico, and I was meeting with some pastors from different churches and denominations.

They told me, "You know, Fernando, some people came from the United States and offered a 3-day class to teach about the Holy Spirit. And they were charging $1,600 for each person."

Do you think this is right to be charging that much? And while we were on the subject, they began sharing with me the excesses that some ministers were going to. They were sharing with me their personal experiences. For instance, they would say, "I'm not going to name names, but this famous preacher came. He said he would come to preach the gospel for $200,000 plus half of the offerings."

Now that, to me, is an extreme. Not only that, but he demanded that he stay at the best hotels, in the private suites. Do you think that Paul would have done that? Or Peter? Or even Jesus? I think you know the answer.

These are problems that are happening and beginning to be prevalent in the church in general. We need to be very careful with this. Certainly, the Holy Spirit didn't charge me anything in order to get to know Him.

He is free of charge. Any knowledge I have about the Holy Spirit should be free of charge.

I don't know where you live, but here in Athens sometimes I hear advertisements that have this headline, "I think your life needs to be enriched, and you need to learn how to pray. You need to grow in your spiritual life. Why don't you take this class? It will bless you so much. Just $80 or $100 for a one-day class."

Someone charging me to teach me how to talk to my Father? That is ridiculous. Praying is talking to God. You talk to God the way you talk to your father. You don't need to learn how to pray. It is a natural thing for a child to talk to his or her father. I think we are living in very dangerous times.

> *If anyone teaches a different doctrine and does not agree with the sound words of our Lord Jesus Christ and the teaching that accords with godliness, he is puffed up with conceit and understands nothing. He has an unhealthy craving for controversy and for quarrels about words, which produce envy, dissension, slander, evil suspicions, and constant friction among people who are depraved in mind and deprived of the truth, imagining that godliness is a means of gain.*
>
> 1 Timothy 6:3-5

If people are trying to charge you for anything that belongs to God, run away as fast and far as you can! Because that's what Paul said to Timothy—depart from such!

> *For we brought nothing into this world, and it is certain we can carry nothing out.*
>
> 1 Timothy 6:7 KJV

Church leadership, pastors, great evangelists, big denominations all have to repent of this sin that is so pervasive in the church. Again, Jesus is going to judge, and it is not going to be pretty.

Diluting the True Message of the Gospel

Lately, during my travels to South America and Latin America, I began to notice that there was a fever within the leadership. Everybody wanted to be an apostle. I called this "apostle-itis." We are greedy and like to have power over people. This is exactly what is taking place around the world. I think God is restoring the perfect five-fold ministry from Ephesians 4 at this time. With that are also emerging the false apostles that the Word describes.

> *For such are false apostles, deceitful workers, transforming themselves into apostles of Christ. And no wonder! For Satan, himself transforms himself into an angel of light. Therefore, it is no great thing if his ministers also transform themselves into ministers of righteousness, whose end will be according to their works.*
>
> 2 Corinthians 11:13-15 KJV

There is an obsession to be called an apostle by someone else. You will usually see the title of 'Apostle' preceding their name. Why do we need to do this? To me, clearly, it is because of arrogance. Perhaps a good example to use for a genuine apostle is the life of Paul. He was always humble. Paul identifies himself as a sinner, and he even calls himself the chief of all sinners (1 Timothy 1:15).

One of the first signs of a true apostle will be the fruit of the Holy Spirit in his life because his character has to be perfect before God.

> *But the fruit of the Spirit is love, joy, peace, patience, kindness, goodness, faithfulness, gentleness, self-control; against such things, there is no law.*
>
> Galatians 5:22

Second, he has to have the signs of an apostle. Miracles, wonders, healing, and the power of the Holy Spirit were always with the apostles. There has to be a balance between the anointing and power and the character that comes from the Holy Spirit. This has to be very, very noticeable in the lives of the so-called apostles. We need the true apostles of the Church, and we need to be able to discern the true apostles from the fake.

A true apostle is one who should be able to work to make a living. Paul worked hard with his hands and provided for himself because he didn't want to be a burden to the church or the believers. False apostles will always be looking to make money, offering "coverage" to and receiving "tithes" from pastors and churches without caring if they are being a burden to the church or not.

Look at the life of Paul. His life was not an easy one. He did not live a luxurious lifestyle. He did not dress in the latest fashion or wear rings and watches of gold. He didn't enjoy any of these things. Instead, the life of Paul was one of persecution, suffering, and lack of necessities. But in all these, he was rich because the Holy Spirit was with him all the time.

Look at the person who says he is an apostle. What is his character like? What standard of living does he have? You will be able to see clearly where his heart is. A true apostle must have a good reputation where his family is concerned. We have to be witnesses to this world of the goodness, grace, and mercy of God.

We need to be able to discern a true apostle from a false apostle. We need to look. So many people say, "Don't judge," but Jesus said we need to look at the fruit. If a tree is giving good fruit, it is a good tree. If not, it is going to be burned in hell (Matthew 7:15-20). Beware, Church, because these are men who have no conscience. They are taking advantage of the things of God, and they are destroying lives.

An apostle is a man that is going to be like a father to you. He will never ask from you, but he will always give to you. In the natural realm, as a father, I never ask my children to provide for me. I am always providing for my children. That is the true heart of the apostle—someone who is always going to provide for his family.

This so-called apostle, how much time do you spend with him? How much advice does he give you? How much does he love you? Clearly, you will be able to see who is a true apostle, and who is not.

Apostles exist, but there are few. From the people I know, I would call a very few true apostles. It is a great calling to be an apostle, but it implies a lot of responsibility and sacrifice that not everyone is willing to make. Church, beware of the false ministers. Do not be deceived, thinking that they are going to cover your life. The only coverage you need is the coverage of the Holy Spirit.

Woe to the rebellious children, saith the LORD, that take counsel, but not of me; and that cover with a covering, but not of my spirit, that they may add sin to sin:

Isaiah 30:1 KJV

If you need counsel, you need to go to God Himself. If you need coverage, you need to go to God Himself. Don't look for a man. Look for Jesus. Look for His Holy Spirit, and your life will be rewarded with blessings, life, peace, and joy. You will be under His shadow, totally protected and nourished (Psalm 91:4).

The Gospel that we are accustomed to hearing now is a diluted message because everything is centered around man. The needs of man. The desires of man. The wishes of man. The dreams of man. As a matter of fact, I think we have taken Jesus out of the church and placed every emphasis on man. Our meetings in churches have become social gatherings, no more, no less, in which the pastors do everything possible to please man.

They worry about the comfort of the seats, how good the atmosphere is, whether it is hot or cold. They also worry about how long the service is going to take, and they look for input through surveys from the church to see what kind of songs people like and how many songs they should sing during the service. The sermon is tailored to please man and to appease someone that's not happy. The pastor is worried about and obsessed with not losing any members because every member that leaves represents how much money they will not receive for a budget.

So we begin to have big problems because this pastor decided to build this huge church, hoping to have a megachurch, and now he has to make larger payments every month. He wants people because he needs money, and he uses the gospel to attract people. It becomes an unending cycle that is centered on the needs of the pastor and the needs of the church.

I have been to churches that have very nice seats so I won't get tired of sitting for too long, and when the worship begins, they dim the lights, so nobody is going to be seen worshipping or not worshipping. They are very concerned with privacy. The lights come up, they put fog around the stage, and the worship team comes in and begins to entertain us with a concert that is based on popular songs. The sermon is always about feeling good or about prosperity and blessings.

We have forgotten the true gospel. The true gospel is based on the desires of a King, the needs of a King. The dreams of a Lord. The gospel is centered on Christ alone.

I ask this question, "What are we going to do with these buildings that we are building and spending millions and millions of dollars upon when Jesus Christ comes?" What will they be good for? I think the answer is obvious.

Jesus Christ is not impressed with our buildings or songs or our sound equipment, lights, and shows. He is impressed with a humble heart, a pure heart. He is impressed with someone that wants to do only His will all the time, someone willing to die for him. Obviously, we don't preach this any longer.

Jesus was very clear when he said, "If they persecuted me, they will persecute you. If they hated me, they will hate you" (John 15:20).

These sermons are not popular now. But I ask you this: How did Jesus die? How did the apostles die? With smiles on their faces? They lived lives of suffering. As a matter of fact, Jesus said,

> *Blessed are you when they revile and persecute you and say all kinds of evil against you falsely for My sake. Rejoice and be exceedingly glad, for great is your reward in heaven, for so they persecuted the prophets who were before you.*
>
> Matthew 5:11-12

Jesus was talking about persecution, and the thing we fear most in the West is persecution. We don't like to talk about this. We don't like to preach about this. Paul considered it an honor to suffer for Christ.

The true gospel is, "If you believe in Me, deny yourself, take up your cross and follow Me" (Luke 9:23).

You know why? Because it is going to cost you everything you have—even your life.

> *If anyone comes to me and does not hate his own father and mother and wife and children and brothers and sisters, yes, and even his own life, he cannot be my disciple.*
>
> Luke 14:26

But we don't want to talk about this. We are always talking about things that we perceive as happy and nice. Jesus also said that if you die before giving your life to Him, you will go to hell and be condemned for your sins (John 3:18). Jesus spoke about hell more than anyone else. You know why? Because it is a reality that the church is trying to ignore in these times. But it is the gospel. If you don't repent and come to Christ, you will go to hell. And hell is not a nice place either.

> *Make every effort to enter through the narrow door, because many, I tell you, will try to enter and will not be able to. Once the owner of the house gets up and closes the door, you will stand outside knocking and pleading, "Sir, open the door for us."*
>
> *But he will answer, "I don't know you or where you come from." Then you will say, "We ate and drank with you, and you taught in our streets." But he will reply, "I don't know you or where you come from. Away from me, all you evildoers!"*
>
> **There will be weeping there, and gnashing of teeth, when you see Abraham, Isaac and Jacob and all the prophets in the kingdom of God, but you yourselves thrown out.**
>
> Luke 13:24-28
>
> *Enter by the narrow gate. For the gate is wide and the way is easy that leads to destruction, and those who enter by it are many. For the gate is narrow and the way is hard that leads to life, and those who find it are few.*
>
> Matthew 7:13-14

CHAPTER 21

THE CHALLENGE OF GOD TO HIS CHURCH

> *The chief danger that confronts the coming century will be religion without the Holy Ghost, Christianity without Christ, forgiveness without repentance, salvation without regeneration, politics without God, heaven without hell.*
> —William Booth, founder of The Salvation Army

Every morning when I wake up, I hear about violence, wars, murders—sins that show the world is getting worse and worse. It seems there is no good news to be found. We are living in very confusing and perilous times, so the future seems very bleak.

The question is, what will the future bring? I am afraid we don't have very good news. When Jesus spoke about the future, He spoke about doom in very graphic terms. In Matthew 24, He began to talk about His second coming and the end of this age. He began with "Take heed that no one deceives you." He said that many would come in His name, saying, "I am the Christ" and deceive many (Matthew 24:5).

I think this phenomenon is beginning to happen over and over again. He said that we will hear of wars and rumors of wars. He told us not to be troubled because all these things must come to pass, but the end is not yet.

> *For nation will rise against nation, and kingdom against kingdom, and there will be famines and earthquakes in various places.*
> Matthew 24:7

He said all of this would be just the beginning of sorrows. I think we are witnessing the beginning of sorrows because of the violence and the wars that are being fought right now.

Then in verse 9, Jesus said, "They will deliver you to tribulation and kill you, and you will be hated by all nations for my name's sake."

Now, this is not a very popular verse. Jesus was saying in clear terms what will happen to the Church. He is talking about the future, and

He is saying it WILL happen. He is talking about a dark time in which persecution is going to be all over the world against Christians and against the church.

> *Many will be offended and will betray one another and will hate one another. Then many false prophets will rise up and deceive many. And because of this, lawlessness will abound, and the love of many will grow cold. But he who endures until the end will be saved. And this gospel of the Kingdom will be preached throughout the world as a witness to all the nations, and then the end will come.*
>
> Matthew 24:10-13 NKJV

The future is bleak, but it is also very glorious. In the midst of worldwide persecution against the Church, the Gospel will be preached to the ends of the earth. So far, the Gospel has not been preached under persecution worldwide, but this is about to come. Believers in the United States will be persecuted. Believers in Europe, Latin America, Africa, and all over the world will be persecuted as well.

We need to be ready because this will come to pass. These are not my words, but these are the words of Jesus. He spoke clearly about the end times.

In my understanding, the Church that we know today will not be able to survive this persecution. The help and the leadership of the Holy Spirit are necessary in order to survive these times. The Church will have to be united because we will not be able to survive; we are so divided. Our minds have to be changed. We won't be able to have public meetings in big churches and buildings. We need to understand that we must go back to house churches, where we can become family and share the love of Jesus Christ.

The restoration of the Church will take place. The Holy Spirit is going back to the first model when the early church was born. The meetings took place in houses. The early church was made up of house churches, and the power, grace, and anointing of the Holy Spirit were present in every meeting. When we talk about the future, we need to see the past. That's what restoration means; you can only restore things that have previously existed, not things that are new.

When the early church was born after Pentecost, it was perfect in every way. If you compare the Church today with the early church after

Pentecost, you will see little similarity. And yet, the Holy Spirit is going to restore His Church.

One day, while I was flying over Mexico City, I saw how big the city is because you fly for literally ten minutes over this city, filled with millions of people. I was praying for revival to come to Mexico City. The first thought that came to my mind was, "Where are we going to put 20 million people? There is no stadium or church or place big enough to put all these people."

And then I heard the Holy Spirit telling me, "Yes, you are right. But I assure you that there are 20 million homes below."

The more I travel, the more I see that the Holy Spirit is going in that direction. House gatherings are going to be vital if we are going to survive the persecution that will prevent believers from gathering in public facilities. During the persecution, you won't care very much about what denomination your brother or sister is in or which church they go to. The only thing that will matter is whether or not they are a believer. Believers without denominations, getting together in houses, growing together in God.

I don't think in the times that are coming that we are going to have time for theology classes and ministries. The only time we are going to have is to preach the Gospel, and I think in the midst of so much violence and death and darkness, the grace of God is going to be manifested, and the last outpouring of the Holy Spirit is going to take place.

This time, Jesus is going to use His Church fully. Everyone is going to be an instrument in the hands of the Holy Spirit. That is the Gospel that is going to be preached around the world. A Gospel that is going to be inspired by the Word of God and confirmed by the Holy Spirit with signs, wonders, and power.

The world will see that Jesus is alive, and He is coming very soon. This Church is going to be powerful, full of believers that are committed to following Jesus. They won't be afraid to die or to lose their houses, cars, jobs, or families. Their only goal and motivation will be to do the will of God and to bring glory to the name of Jesus. That's the generation that God is raising up. They will see the glory of God in the fullest.

In the Western hemisphere, the Church has been focusing too much on the last outpouring of the Holy Spirit, how God is going to move, and the glory that we are going to see. This is correct, but we don't want to talk about the persecution and suffering that already exists in the rest of the Church in different parts of the world. Our brothers and sisters in China, Korea, Africa, the Middle East, even Europe, at this time are going through persecution. We need to understand what is coming here, and the Church needs to be ready.

> *After this I looked, and behold, a great multitude that no one could number, from every nation, from all tribes and peoples and languages, standing before the throne and before the Lamb, clothed in white robes, with palm branches in their hands, and crying out with a loud voice, "Salvation belongs to our God who sits on the throne, and to the Lamb!"*
>
> *Then one of the elders addressed me, saying, "Who are these, clothed in white robes, and from where have they come?" I said to him, "Sir, you know." And he said to me, "These are the ones coming out of the great tribulation. They have washed their robes and made them white in the blood of the Lamb.*
>
> Revelation 7:9-10, 12-14

Are you ready?

The only purpose that Jesus had when He was on earth was to do the will of God, which was to redeem man. He was willing to do everything—even to lay His life down at the cross. I think that needs to be our attitude. We have to surrender to God. We need to be able to surrender our own agendas and be willing to pay the price. Perhaps our attitude can be "I'm willing to serve You, in spite of the cost. I'm willing to do anything and everything to preach Your gospel, to do Your will and Your purpose for Your name to be glorified."

Now, we do not have the time nor the luxury to live an idle life, where Christianity is going to church for an hour and a half every weekend and praying twice a week and reading the Bible here and there, while searching for the riches of this world, looking out always for our wellbeing. I think this time is over. Times are changing. Either you are with Jesus, or you are against Him. Either you are hot, or you are cold. You cannot be in the middle anymore. Your life has to be dedicated entirely to Christ in order for you to survive the times that are coming to this earth.

Bolivia should be an example of this because of the events that have unfolded lately concerning the government and the church.

I will raise up this man to challenge My Church.

This prophecy has been fulfilled at this time.

See, Jesus told us that times are going to be hard—however, we have the consolation that the Holy Spirit is with us. He is the one who is going to give us the strength and wisdom we need to endure. He is the one who is going to teach us, guide us, and give us comfort and His anointing to preach the gospel. He will enable us to live according to the gospel.

As you can see, we need the Holy Spirit more than ever before. Only with Him are we going to be able to survive these times that are coming. But we should lift up our heads and rejoice because our Lord and King is coming very soon!

Yes, Jesus is coming soon.

BIBLIOGRAPHY

Liardon, Roberts. "David du Plessis." *God's Generals*, Roberts Liardon Ministries, godsgenerals.com/davidplessis/.

Nicky Cruz. "Chapter 17: Beating the Devil." *Satan on the Loose*, Fleming H. Revell Company, 1973, pp. 131–144.

Ortuño, President of the Republic General René Barrientos. "A New Homeland Dynamics." *Move from Theoretical Nationalism to Integral Development*, pp. 7–9. Institutional Repository UMSA, repositorio.umsa.bo/bitstream/handle/123456789/9389/BC-F-01318.pdf?%20sequence=1&isAllowed=y.

Ruibal, Julio C. *Anointed for the Endtime Harvest*. Julio Ruibal Foundation, 1998.

Zambrana, Orlando Murillo. "Education in Bolivia: Indicators, Figures and Results." pp. 34-36. Organization of American States, Ministry of Education, Bolivia, 2004, https://web.oas.org/childhood/ES/Lists/Recursos%20%20Planes%20Nacionales/Attachments/19/3.%20La%20educación%20en%20Bolivia,%20Indicadores,%20Cifras%20y%20Resultados.pdf

ABOUT THE AUTHOR

Fernando Villalobos encountered the love of Christ as a teenager during a spiritual revival that transformed the nation of Bolivia through powerful signs and wonders in the 1970s. After receiving a vision of Jesus Christ dying for him on the cross, he surrendered his life to preach the gospel, which he has been preaching throughout the nations of the world ever since. He currently works as a paramedic in Athens, GA, where he lives with his wife, Laura. They have two daughters, one granddaughter, and have become spiritual parents to countless others through opening their home and sharing their unique and miraculous experiences. Their meetings have attracted believers and seekers of all ages, nations, races, and walks of life to come and learn about the love, mercy, and unchanging power of God.